Husbands, Wives, God

Introducing Your Marriage to the Marriages of the Bible

Edward Lee

Husbands, Wives, God: Introducing Your Marriage to the Marriages
of the Bible

ISBN 978-0-578-03844-5

To my precious son, Connor Edward Lee. Daddy loves you!!

Trust in the LORD with all your heart and do not lean on your own understanding. In all your ways acknowledge Him, and He will make your paths straight. (Prov. 3:5-6)

Contents

Acknowledgements

All of the credit for the creation and completion of this book goes to my Lord and Savior, Jesus Christ, who died for me and saved me even before the foundation of this world.

My pastor, Pastor Kenneth L. Barney, has an old country saying that I thought was odd the first time I heard it, but during the three years that I have been writing this book, I have come to understand it: "Anytime you see a turtle sitting on a fence, realize that someone put it there." Just as turtles don't climb fences by themselves, I would like to thank and acknowledge the very special people that walked alongside me during the creation and writing of this book:

To my beautiful wife Kimber: Without you and what we have learned from and taught each other, this book would never have been possible. Thank you for all the sacrifices you continually make for me and our family, which allow me the time to do God's work. Thank you for being the "balance" that God knows I need.

To my paternal and maternal grandparents, Charles and Corinea Lee, and Sylvester and Thelma Nealy – a deep heart felt Thank You: Even though they are at rest in heaven, the years of love, sacrifice and "modeling" that they offered me so freely continue to give shape to my life, and to this book in particular. They modeled longevity in Christian faith and lived the vow, "'till death do us part," through long standing Christian marriages of forty and fifty-nine years respectively.

Edward Sr. and Janet Lee, a.k.a. Dad and Mom, thanks for forty-three years of modeling their marriage commitment. To my father—a perennial student, educator, handyman, golf partner, servant of the Lord, and my friend—you taught me the compassionate side of being a man. Mom, I still remember those spring and summer mornings that I would wake early to find you in deep devotion to the Lord, and that image sticks with me to this day. Thank you both for insisting on my choosing reading and writing over basketball.

In many ways, my emphasis on biblical marriages was an out-growth of what I learned from the first couple that I counseled, and whose wedding was the first at which I officiated, my sister Carla Tatum and my brother-in-love, Alvin Tatum, Sr. Special blessings to you both.

To all of the pastors, and their respective ministries, who unsel-fishly helped to grow me in manhood and pastoral soulcare. Since my early days, there have been strong pastors and devoted believers who have mentored and groomed me: Rev. David Minus, Jr. (deceased), formerly of the Second Baptist Church, Pottstown, Pa., who nurtured me and modeled Christian manhood over long talks and lemonade when I was a boy; Rev. Roland Anderson, currently of Second Baptist of Pottstown, who always has a book for me to read; Bishop Claude R. Alexander, University Park Baptist, Charlotte, N.C., thanks is hardly enough—God used your preaching and mentorship through Jesus Christ to cause me to stop running and start serving; and to Pastor Kenneth L. Barney, Sr., New Antioch Baptist Church of Randallstown, Randalls-town, Md., with whom I now serve and grow in ministry, may God continue to bless you, your family, and ministry for all that you have allowed me to see and experience in Christian service. God Bless You All.

Lastly, I want to thank two special people that served as "book-ends" to the writing of this book, Jason Fenwick and Rick Kern. In the early days, Jason and I would meet once a week to bounce ideas off each other and dedicate time to our respective writing projects. I count it a blessing to have a friend who pushes you to stop dreaming and get started. I also acknowledge Rick Kern whom God brought along in year three of the writing of this book. Rick labored in this work for the Lord as a consultant, sounding board, and to be most treasured as a new friend. His enthusiasm and energy breathed freshness into this work.

God Bless you, ALL!

Foreword

I have had the pleasure of working with marriages in various capacities for the last fifteen years. Much of that time has been spent traveling from marriage event to marriage event, hosting prolific ministry leaders such as Dr. Gary Chapman, Drs. Les and Leslie Parrott, and Dr. Gary and Barb Rosberg. Through the course of these ministry travels, I have engaged with hundreds of local churches. Among these hundreds of church programs were *thousands* of methods, manuals, ideas, tips, and tools, all developed to somehow help the married couples in their respective churches.

Don't hear me wrong: I am not against tips and tools for helping married couples. After all, much of what I do at MarriageVine Ministries is designed to help facilitate and communicate these practical helps to married couples! However, it is abundantly clear to me that there is only one true source of wisdom—that is, God and His written word.

Without the understanding of what God says about marriage and relationships, we are left to our own wisdom and then we simply add on the muddled, relativistic ideas of the world's wisdom. Couples must seek to understand The Source of all wisdom and understanding, grace and forgiveness, mercy and love. As followers of Christ, we have God's heart on marriage in written form—and He has much to say!

This is why it is a joy to endorse Edward's good work, *Husbands, Wives, God,* to you with a prayer that you will use it well. For if you do, it will lead you to the *One* who can give you peace amidst your storm, comfort in your darkness, and joy in your perpetual trials—until the day of no more faith, when at last we see our Savior, Jesus the Christ.

Rick Pierce
President
MarriageVine Ministries

Introduction

In *Husbands, Wives, God*, you will be introduced to seven marriages taken straight from the Bible. Just as would be the case if a friend or colleague would introduce you to someone at an event, the idea is that there is something of value to be gained by you and that person meeting each other. Likewise, each of the biblical couples that will be introduced to your marriage offers a *value* to your marriage. These are their stories—woven together to produce changed hearts, attitudes, perspectives, and ultimately, changed marriages. They were selected in order to channel the focus of husbands and wives to the most important relationship that a couple has, a balanced relationship between them and God, hence the book's title, *Husbands, Wives, God.* The premise being that a relationship only between husbands and wives that excludes or minimizes their relationship with God is severely imbalanced and will struggle mightily under life's pressures. However, there is a certain balance or wholeness that is gained in a three party relationship with husbands, wives, and God. It is a relationship that moves couples beyond the typical give-and-take between husbands and wives into interaction with *The Source* of wisdom, guidance, strength, and true lasting love. Along the way, you will meet couples that demonstrated either balance, or a lack of balance, in their relationship with God in the midst of their realities. Culturally and socially, the marriages of the Bible and our own modern marriages are worlds apart; God's teaching and wisdom, however, does not change—ever. Therefore, the marriages within the Bible remain relevant, insightful, and powerful models for marriages today.

Each of these seven marriages endured its unique trials because the couple involved learned, usually through painful processes and circumstances, to shift the strain of their relationship off their four collective shoulders and onto God. The lessons these couples learned remain relevant because, in many marriages today, couple's believe they are doing all that is within their means to maintain or improve their relationship. However, the reality is that the capacity to maintain and/or fix their marriage simply does not exist between a *husband and wife*.

This reality is precisely what makes the marriages of the Bible so important—because as they develop or demonstrate a balanced relationship with *God*, they exceed the natural, human capacities and limitations of *husbands and wives.*

For example, as we will discuss later in the book, when a woman named Leah was married to a man that the Bible describes as hating her, she tried everything within her power to win his love. But eventually, when she had her fill of trying to fix her marriage to no avail, she then decided to focus her attention on God. The result? Well, you'll have to read that chapter. But what about your marriage? Perhaps you and your spouse have reached such a point of exhaustion from trying to "fix" your relationship and are in need of a change. Or perhaps you just want to preserve the relationship you have. Wherever you are in your marriage walk, a *closer* walk with God is in order.

The Development of Husbands, Wives, God

During my thirty-year walk as a Christian, in various lay ministry positions and now in full-time ministry, God has been developing my affinity for studying, teaching and sharing His Word. In recent years, this love for God's Word has been married (no pun intended) with my providing pastoral and biblical counsel to couples inside and outside of the church.

Then, two weeks after my third wedding anniversary, I began serving as the Assistant to the Pastor of New Antioch Baptist Church of Randallstown, on the outskirts of Baltimore, Md.   Among the more substantial aspects of this ministry position was Pastoral Marriage Counseling, through which God continued to develop my understanding of what the Bible teaches about marriage. Initially, I envisioned brushing up on the familiar biblical passages about the roles of husbands and wives in marriage, or what true love is. What I did not expect was to encounter roughly fifty narrative accounts of marriages in the Bible. The accounts of these real marriages from years ago not only defined godly marriage perspectives and behaviors, but also evidenced relationships that endured heartache, flourished during national crises and economic instability, rebuilt trust in spite of adultery, and displayed integrity even when one of the spouses didn't. In essence, these biblical marriages share struggles familiar to ours today.

The book you now hold in your hand and the related marriage resources (ie. Study Guide and Prayer Journal/Devotional) are an outgrowth of the pastoral and biblical counseling that God has allowed me to offer as a lay leader, friend, mentor, coach, and then as an ordained minister, in various settings and capacities, both inside and outside of the church. Regardless of the setting, nature, or scope of the issue, the guiding principles of these two verses have shaped my perspective and thinking:

> For the word of God is living and active and sharper than any two-edged sword, and piercing as far as the division of soul and spirit, of both joints and marrow, and able to judge the thoughts and intentions of the heart. And there is no creature hidden from His sight, but all things are open and laid bare to the eyes of Him with whom we have to do. (Hebrews 4:12-13)

Over the years, in conjunction with my study of biblical marriages, I have read every book about marriage that I could get my hands on. As I did so, I came to realize that only God's Word, the Bible, contains the power to break through years of heartache, disappointment, broken promises, adultery, substance abuse, neglect, denial, and the like. After reading a number of secular and Christian marriage books, it became clear to me through prayer that this was not to be another how-to book about marriage, based on my very limited human advice and biased perspectives. As I tell most couples that I counsel, "My opinions and advice are not strong enough to help get you out of the door." However, what I found that every couple needs, regardless of their condition, is the "meat" of God's Word. It is in the Bible that marriages can find the *balance* that their relationship is need of, the balance of a relationship between a *Husband, Wife, and God.*

Who Is This Book For?

Husbands, Wives, God is intended for any couple desiring a better spousal relationship through a deeper spiritual relationship. Regardless of how bad or good a marriage is, the principles of this book should prove beneficial. The real strength of this book is that it points to the Bible.

Husbands, Wives, God is unashamedly and necessarily rooted in Christian principles and values. However, it has amazed me how God has used the principles found in biblical marriages in some unexpected ways to help those who don't consider themselves to be Christians, religious, or even spiritual. For example, there was a young lady in my gym who did not believe in Jesus or God. During the course of our conversation one day, she haltingly asked for some wisdom about her marriage and so I shared the story of Jacob and Leah with her. Its message left her encouraged and determined to pursue a better relationship with her spouse. Then there was the man I met one day who asked for advice on whether he should choose to stay with his girlfriend or return to his wife. It was through my sharing about the marriage of Adam and Eve that he came to the understanding that he needed to reach out to his wife. I stand convinced that the principles gleaned from biblical marriages can and will strengthen modern-day marriages.

I don't look solely at how sharing biblical marriages has helped others. But I get so excited about lessons absorbed through these marriages because I have seen what they have done for my wife and I. They were a source of confidence, healing, and praise when we were told, "It will be physically impossible for the two of you to have children," (Praise the Lord, our son is now one year old and getting into everything). When we reached flash points in our relationship and our only conversation was an argument, revisiting these biblical marriages gave me a guidepost for communicating with my wife. And when our own individual perspectives were the only consideration in dealing with life and marriage, the marriages that you are going to read about here provided direction. My wife and I have seen the marriages of the Bible deconstruct our individual walls and barriers to then build bridges which allowed us to love each other the way we longed to. It is my prayer that as you embrace the marriages in this book, whatever condition your marriage is in, you and your spouse will be pointed back to God's book, the Bible. For it is only in the Bible that true and lasting healing is waiting for all of *us*.

Enjoy and God Bless You.

Edward

HOW TO USE THIS BOOK:

The principles shared in this book are pastoral and not clinical in nature. As such, the purpose and structure allows couples to look reflectively and introspectively into their marriage and relationship with God individually and as a couple. To provide clarity, at the beginning of each chapter you will find "Marriage Principles in this Chapter." Under this heading are the principles that will be provided in the chapter.

To effectively achieve introspection and ultimately lasting change, every chapter will share the story and lessons of a biblical marriage. Each marriage will prove to be relatable to marriages today.

At the end of selected chapters, there will be a section encouraging you to "Think on These Things: Passages for Further Meditation and Memorization." Here you will find a selection of relevant scriptures to consider in light of your own marriage. Undoubtedly, there will be verses that will impact your marriage in a profound way. It may be that you and your spouse will want to memorize them together so that, in the heat of the moment, they provide a safeguard against ill-spoken words, deeds, or thoughts. As will be pointed out, this is an invaluable practice that will bless your marriage. So I encourage you, as you and your spouse come in contact with other relevant passages, to make note of them, talk about them, and memorize them.

Also at the end of chapters, there will be a "Talking Points" section. These questions are intended to generate deeper thought about and introspection of a couple's particular relationship. Except where otherwise suggested, the questions are intended for couples to discuss together. The more open a couple can be when thinking through and discussing these questions, the more effective the lessons of the chapters will become.

Lastly, after the last chapter there is a small group and Bible study guide. This is intended primarily for churches and marriage ministries. But of course, any group of any size will find it a suitable resource to foster deeper conversation among couples.

Chapter One

Abraham and Sarah:
The Model Marriage

Marriage Principles in this Chapter:
- Exercising Faith in God
- Exercising Obedience in Marriage
- Exercising a Godly Perspective in Marriage

*W*HEN A RUNNER LINES up for a race, it is the vision of the finish line that puts the determined look on her face as she waits for the "pow" of the starting gun. When a sculptor looks at a formless lump of clay, it is the grandeur of its final form that his mind's eye delights in and his hands reach for. And when a writer sits, pen in hand, beholding the blank page in front of him, it is the last page that he envisions turning, with the end of the book in the front of his mind.

Similarly, when a man and woman stand at the altar and gaze intently into one another's eyes, their minds are flooded with a guiding vision of blissfully growing old together. Perchance your own marriage started out with a similar vision of your life together—a vision of wedded bliss, long walks, good times, great passionate nights, raising great kids: a good life together. However, what typically is obscured from view on "that" side of the "I do" are the magnitude, effect and resulting scars of the inevitable pressures and disappointments along the way. As the years of marriage march on, those once blurry tough times come sharply into focus and cloud a once clear picture.

In this first chapter I want to introduce you to a reliable "model" of marital durability that abides amid the pressures and difficulties that can weigh on a marriage. It is a couple that can model love in the trials of life because their own love has been guided by godly influences. Having a good model for your marriage will not guarantee that there will never be hard times or a rough spot in your marriage; some measure of pressure is unavoidable and, to an extent, needed. But a model can become a compass that leads toward balance when life blurs a couple's vision. Both personally and through sharing biblical marriages with couples, I have come to realize that in order to obtain, regain, or maintain a healthy marriage, couples will be served well by having other couples who function as role models for their marriage— either positively or negatively.

Personally, I have kept a mental picture of my maternal grandparents, Sylvester and Thelma Nealy, both now at rest with the Lord, firmly in my mind. What I remember about their marriage continually helps me develop as a husband and, at times, has helped to pull my perspective of myself and/or my marriage back in line. For fifty-nine years, they had a marriage that was balanced by their relationship with God. It was not a perfect relationship, but it was a God-centered relationship that began every morning with prayer, Bible reading, and talking openly. My grandmother, for her part, could make the best lemon meringue pie this side of heaven, but she could also be a "little" feisty toward my grandfather. Yet, my memory of my grandfather is that whenever tensions would rise between him and my grandmother, rather than losing his temper or expressing unkindness, he would slip away to a quiet room, close his eyes, twiddle his thumbs, and begin to pray. Within a few minutes, he would return to the family gathering with a gentle, quiet, and peace-filled disposition. It was this sort of godly temperament that allowed them to build a marriage that could endure life's challenges.

There were also the occasions where, regardless of what his personal agenda was for the day (usually working in his garden), he would pause to drive my grandmother wherever she needed to go. In fact, I don't really ever remember my grandmother driving anywhere. As a child and teenager, I thought his servitude was at times silly. I mean, she had her own car and was able to drive; he just did it for her. Now I understand that what he was doing was modeling the attitude of a biblical husband by serving his wife, often despite his feelings. It was his way of modeling marital balance not based on a fifty-fifty split with my grandmother, but on his relying one hundred percent on the Lord. My grandfather's eyes were on the Lord more than on his wife, and that focus enabled him to be a servant to her and all of his family.

In later years, after my grandfather passed away, my grandmother and I became very close. She would often reflect on how the Lord kept their marriage through so many trying times. She would tell of the difficulties they experienced as an African-American couple traveling from Pennsylvania to Florida in the 1950s and 60s with two small children, and yet unable to get a hotel or use the restroom as they passed through the Southern states. The wistful look in her eyes was precious as she recalled how they learned to make fun and find joy in life's painful realities. It was in how they handled "life" that the depth of their total, unreserved reliance on God spoke to me as a child, and speaks into my own marriage to this very day.

My grandparents did not have tons of money. My grandfather worked building ships in a naval shipyard in Philadelphia, and my grandmother was a seamstress. But they had a love for their vows to God that surpassed the difficulties they faced. One day in the 1980s, my grandfather was working on the lawnmower in the basement and some of the gasoline trickled out and made it over to the furnace. As he reached to clean it up, the furnace exploded, just inches from his face. The force of the blast was so powerful that it knocked down my grandmother who was two stories away, on the second floor. Yet my grandfather, who was just inches from the blast, walked away from their demolished house completely unscathed.

The explosion was totally his fault but, because of their mutual focus on the Lord, there was never a moment of blame. Nor was there any noticeable strain on their marriage. But once again they seemed to grow stronger as a result of facing adversity together. And during the year they spent cramped in a small two-bedroom apartment waiting for their three-bedroom/two-story house to be rebuilt, there was never any mention of animosity or bickering. To me it looked like they enjoyed living in those cramped quarters—because for whatever material possessions they had lost, they still had the love of one another.

As I reflect on my grandparents' marriage and their ability to weather so many storms through their fifty-nine years together, what is imprinted on my mind is not only the inclusion of God in their relationship, but their absolute and total dependence on Him. Their relationship with God was deeper than just going to church, or paying lip service. Beyond their personal resources, wisdom, and perspective—beyond it all, God was the fulcrum around which their marriage turned. It was their ability to model their behavior, perspectives, and love for each other after what they saw in the Bible that gave shape to their love.

In this book (as well as the accompanying study guide and the Husbands, Wives, God Prayer Journal and Devotional), we will identify biblical marriages that provide clear models to follow: with two autonomous people in love, each dependent on the other, and both dependent upon God, balanced and poised as one flesh, to handle the pressures that will confront them during their relationship. Without these godly pictures of marriage to look to, hills can quickly look like mountains, potholes can feel like valleys, and times of distance can resemble being abandoned in the desert. However, developing a reliable picture or model of marital health will serve the relationship well during the rise of inevitable pressures.

Usually how a husband and wife treat each other is a direct result of what has been modeled before their eyes either during childhood or through life experiences. Therefore in this opening chapter I want to introduce you to the reliable biblical "model" of Abraham and Sarah for all couples to look to. This couple from the Bible "models" the ability to endure pressure, setbacks, harsh realities, and disappointments in marriage. They maintained their harmony and balance in the face of intense trials and great disappointments—a balance that did not come from their energy reserves, financial status, or any other attribute rooted in time or secular life. Instead, it emerged solely from the quality of their individual relationships with God, and it bound them together.

Countless times, I have seen couples admire other marriages based on what they observe from their vantage point. Therefore, they desire the quality relationship that they perceive someone else to have, only to discover that the couple they thought had a perfect marriage actually was in worse shape than they were. Thankfully, however, through the marriage of Abraham and Sarah, God provides a durable, quality relationship model that is both desirable and attainable for us because of who they were inside, more than who they appeared to be on the outside. One's earning capacity, the ability to gain material "things," even to raise great children or reside in a big house, was never meant to be emblematic of a quality marriage. Instead, a great relationship is found in the quality of our character, which only God can see, but is not in the full view of our peers (cf. reference to Sarah in 1 Peter 3:1-7).

As I present Abraham and Sarah as having the model marriage, be careful not to confuse their marriage with a perfect marriage. The mistakes, faults, and blemishes of this couple are as evident as they are in any other relationship. They tell lies, display lapses of faith, and even laugh at God. Simultaneously, they demonstrate faith, obedience, a godly perspective, and are memorialized in what is referred to as the *Hall of Faith* (Hebrews, Ch. 11). It is this strange mix of high character and low roads that allows them to maintain a realistic equilibrium between themselves and God.

The other marriages shared in this book will have some of the same qualities that made Abraham and Sarah's marriage successful. In some places they may even seem to overlap the principles used by Abraham and Sarah, but few if any will portray their overall marital health. To that end, I introduce to your marriage the reliable model of Abraham and Sarah, with their unwavering and indomitable faith in God when faced with circumstances that would prove insurmountable to most.

Abraham and Sarah: A Husband, A Wife, God

Together, Abraham and Sarah faced a collage of demanding situations. Although they didn't handle all of their challenges the "right" way, their relationship with God enabled them to endure life's challenges. In spite of the tough times they faced, their relationship with God gave them the capacity to be woven together in a lasting, resilient, and refreshing relationship. Apart from their relationship with God, it is difficult to conceive that their marriage would have had the degree of durability that is witnessed in their marriage.

Theirs is a story originally portrayed in the biblical text between Genesis 12, when Abraham is called to follow God, to Genesis 25, when he dies. However, Abraham and Sarah are such central figures to the overall story of the Bible that they are referred to multiple times throughout the scriptures. Rather than address every instance in which they are referred to in the Bible, we will instead use the portrait painted of Abraham and Sarah in chapter 11 of the Book of Hebrews as the central point of our discussion. Throughout the accounts of their marriage, there are three distinct traits of their relationship with God that provide us a valuable model for our own marriages.

#1 - Exercising Faith in God

The first distinguishing trait of their relationship is *faith* in God. It is said in Romans 4:3 that faith is what made Abraham a righteous man in the sight of God: "For what does the Scripture say? 'ABRAHAM BELIEVED GOD, AND IT WAS CREDITED TO HIM AS RIGHTEOUSNESS.'"

Faith goes beyond a simple confession of Christ devoid of conviction, or just attending church, faith is about a trust relationship in God's ability to act on our behalf through the seen and unseen trials of life. When we are either certain or uncertain about what direction we are to take, how we are to respond to life, or how trials will get resolved, we must exercise faith. It is faith that empowers us to relinquish the reliance on our own ability and to place it squarely and confidently on the shoulders of God. Here are five clear and commanding points that Hebrews 11 makes about faith's ability to shift the reliance from "us" to God:

1. By faith, we **understand** how God made the world, i.e., "Let there be light" (cf. Heb. 11:3 and Gen. 1:3).
2. Faith tells us that all that was made (i.e., nature) was **made not from visible things** but invisible things (Heb. 11:3).

3. Faith tells us that God rewards those that *diligently seek Him*, as opposed to exercising their own logic or reasoning (cf. Heb. 11:6).
4. Absence of this trust relationship with God makes it *impossible to please God* (cf. Heb. 11:6).
5. People *gain approval* from God through faith (Heb. 11:2).

These points do not speak directly to marriage but their truths are applicable to every situation that a person faces. Therefore, they go a long way to explaining the power of a couple's faith to understand what can not be seen or readily understood in their marriage. When experiencing dissatisfaction and rough patches, they provide a reservoir of strength and a reason to endure that far exceeds our own logic and sheer willpower. I sum up the power of the trust relationship that a couple gains by faith like this: An unshakable trust in God's ability to illumine the darkness that envelops our hearts and minds when hurt and disappointment cloud our picture of marital bliss.

Abraham and Sarah demonstrate this unshakable reliance in God beyond their own abilities, in Hebrews 11:8-10, which retells the events of Genesis 12:1-5.

> By faith Abraham, when he was called, obeyed by going out to a place which he was to receive for an inheritance; and he went out, not knowing where he was going. By faith he lived as an alien in the land of promise, as in a foreign land, dwelling in tents with Isaac and Jacob, fellow heirs of the same promise; for he was looking for the city which has foundations, whose architect and builder is God.

In this passage, Abraham was called by God to leave his homeland, family, and all that was familiar to him, and go to an undisclosed land that God would show him at some point in the future. Then for a period of years, he dwelt as a fish out of water, separated from all that was familiar to him, in this land that God had promised him. During these years, he could live among strangers because his faith enabled him to look beyond the comforts of the city and familiar surroundings and to trust that God would provide a heavenly city—a city superior to any earthly city he was accustomed to. His reliance on the city God would lead them to exceeded his reliance on what his own logic or resources could provide for him. And Abraham did all of this with his wife and everything they owned in tow. What an extreme exercise of faith in God on the part of Abraham and Sarah!

Imagine for a minute if your employer asked you to put your house on the market, pack everything into a U-Haul truck, and move your family away from everything you and they are comfortable with. Oh, and only once you have packed and actually started drive away will your boss reveal your destination. Most would say Thanks, but no thanks. We would not move until we had more specific details about where we were going. However, Abraham and Sarah were fueled by a faith in and reliance on God's provision, even without being privy to all the details. Through this reliance on God, they gained a foundation of strength to leave the familiar and go into the unknown. Their faith provided the insight to look beyond their comfort zone and circum-stances, and to venture through human reason to trust the call of God. What a remarkable modeling of reliance upon God beyond what many would call logical. I don't imagine that the call of God to go into the unknown generated any less anxiety than our own unknown journey does. No one really knows what the next moments, days, months, or years will bring. But with our eyes fixed more on heaven, than relying on what is seen on earth, we too can gain strength to endure life's journey. It really is like a launching pad, it is their solid foundation of faith that enables them to rise up in the face of life's uncertainties. This faith model of Abraham and Sarah provides a really good point of reflection. In difficult times, what do you have to rely on? So far beyond the limitations of their earthly resources, which would leave any of us feeling helpless, Abraham and Sarah had the inexhaustible resources of God to rely upon.

However, the other side of the coin is that after they left and dis-played this great faith in God, Abraham succumbs to his fear of the people who live in the land of Egypt (cf. Genesis 12:10-16). In this instance, he asks his wife to lie and say that she is his sister, not his wife, so they won't kill him. So, on one hand—great faith; on the other hand—lack of faith. It is a reminder that faith is not something to be grasped or stored up, but rather, it is to be exercised in the face of "life." The faith that Abraham and Sarah used to get up and go, into the unfamiliar was nowhere to be found just a short time later when encountering the Egyptians. When a seemingly less threatening situation arose, they pulled matters back into their own hands and displayed a lack of faith.

Likewise, in modern relationships, husbands and wives tend to pick and choose when and with what to trust God. However, the marriage able to endure its share of pressures rises to the daily challenge to exercise faith in God's ability beyond the abilities and resources of man and woman. It is a challenge that is met in the great and small scenes of life. Exercise is such an appropriate word here because, just as neglecting to exercise our physical bodies results in negative results, neglecting to exercise faith has negative effects on our marriages. Just as is evidenced with Abraham and Sarah the exercise of faith yields great strength and endurance. On the other hand failure to exercise faith renders the couple susceptible to fear, anxiety and stress. Every day that God gives a couple to spend together provides a new opportunity to exercise their faith in God. Past points of faithfulness cannot be stored for future challenges, but on a daily basis husbands and wives must exercise faith in and reliance on God.

#2 - Exercising Obedience in Marriage

As an outgrowth of their faith in God, Abraham and Sarah's marriage models *obedience*. Not so much obedience to each other but to God. It is a trait which strengthens their interaction and connection as husband and wife. By obedience it is meant that they lived in line with God's authority. Their obedience is captured in the same Hebrews 11:8 and Genesis 12 passages in which we saw their display of faith. Let's take a look at the account of Abraham and Sarah in Genesis 12:1-5:

> Now the LORD said to Abram, "Go forth from your country, And from your relatives And from your father's house, To the land which I will show you; And I will make you a great nation, And I will bless you, And make your name great; And so you shall be a blessing; And I will bless those who bless you, And the one who curses you I will curse And in you all the families of the earth will be blessed." *So Abram went forth as the LORD had spoken to him;* and Lot went with him. Now

Abram was seventy-five years old when he departed from Haran. Abram took Sarai his wife and Lot his nephew, and all their possessions which they had accumulated, and the persons which they had acquired in Haran, and they set out for the land of Canaan; thus they came to the land of Canaan. (emphasis added)

Again, as we saw in the last section, in this passage God tells Abraham to leave everything that is comfortable and familiar—just get moving and I will give you further instruction in my own time as you go. God spoke to Abraham and he obeyed, but we cannot overlook that as he determined to obey God's words to him, Sarah went with him. It is the Bible's lack of any mention of protest on Sarah's part that testifies to her obedience. She simply obeys the voice of God as spoken to her husband. It was a voice that was recognizable to her because she knew God for herself. It is a dual display of obedience that enables them to leave comfort and familiarity for the unknown. While God may not prove your obedience to Him, or test the strength of your marriage by asking you to leave your country and comfort zone, hard-hitting circumstances are bound to intrude into your marriage, requiring unshakable obedience to the voice of God in very scary times.

It is here, in the uncomfortable times of marriage, more than anywhere else, that the depth of love and blessing experienced by two wedded hearts, beating as one, hinges on their obedience to God. It is here that obedience becomes a door that either opens the path to spiritual intimacy, bringing husband and wife closer together, or shuts it out, estranging them from one another. God tells them, once they leave home, nation, and family, that then and only then will God make Abraham a great nation, bless him, make his name great, allow him to be a blessing, curse anyone that curses him, and bless all the families of the earth through Abraham. Imagine the strain and misery their marriage could have been saddled with, had Abraham not obeyed God's call to leave his country? Or if Sarah would have decided that she did not want to follow where God was leading her husband? Instead, thousands of years later, we still discuss this model of obedience seen in the marriage of Abraham and Sarah. I like to be very careful and avoid over-promising or bending the scriptures to say something they really don't. But what these passages declare is what Abraham actually went through, and in his own obedience and subsequently his wife's too, they are mightily blessed by God. While the circumstances that you face may differ greatly, the point remains that your relationship with your spouse flourishes or withers in direct proportion to obedience to God.

Similar to the power gained by exercising faith, obedience also shifts the responsibility from husband and wife to God. The responsibility of an obedient couple is to follow, not to provide answers. There are 1,000 logical reasons why they should not leave their home and go into unknown circumstance and only one reason why they should leave–God told them to. In like manner, as you and your spouse come in contact with God through His word in the Bible there is a call to be obedient to what is read and seen. As you exercise obedience to God, you begin to gain a balance to face the unknowns of life together.

#3 - Exercising a Godly Perspective in Marriage

In addition to their extraordinary faith in God and their obedience to Him, Abraham and Sarah model the durability of their marriage by exercising a godly perspective in Hebrews 11:9-10:

> By faith he lived as an alien in the land of promise, as in a foreign land, dwelling in tents with Isaac and Jacob, fellow heirs of the same promise; for he was looking for the city which has foundations, whose architect and builder is God.

I encounter many couples that are being tripped up by their perspective of how marriage is or should be. We'll go into this in more detail when we look at the marriage of Adam and Eve. But, while Abraham and Sarah have us here, we can see that their perspectives were shaped by their view of God, more than by their life experiences. After they allowed their faith in and obedience to God to lead them to an unknown land, Abraham and his wife lived in tents as strangers in a foreign land. This is so very countercultural to the normal perspective of life, especially married life. This couple gave up their mainstays of security, an address, land, and relatives, for life on the road in a tent!! And they did so because they had a heavenly perspective.

All marriages at times are susceptible to looking inward to their human feelings, ideals, rationales and principles, allowing those to dominate the sense of peace, joy, and stability that couples desire. But here is a couple, in Abraham and Sarah, who focused on an unchanging God rather than on the difficulty of the unstable situation they found themselves in. In so doing, they endured their difficulty and triumphed through their circumstances.

In a modern sense, the cliché, "he who has the most toys, wins," rings truer than ever, and the health and stability of a couple is so often assessed by the material things they accumulate during their relationship. Probably foremost in this assessment are their house and family. But this couple saw through the recklessness of such illegitimate values and found their own sense of balance in God. Their perspective in leaving their comfort, then ending up in a foreign land, was to focus on a holy city built by God. For God had promised Abraham spiritual blessings, which became the prize he kept his eye on. Theirs was a stability not built on an earthly frame of reference, but on a heavenly one.

In many modern marriages husbands and wives are bowed beneath the weight of some sense of loss, whether material or intangible: a job, house, financial stability, trust, respect, and the like. Whatever the loss, the foundation of the relationship is violently shaken. But the lesson that Abraham and Sarah personify is that in the inevitable and necessary losses of life, there is a heavenly perspective resting on the bedrock of eternal truth that is absolutely unshakeable. And as we rest our hearts on it, we can know that there are things that this world did not give us, so it cannot steal them from us. This is not to say that in our marriages we are to deny hurts and pains, or any other reality, for that matter. Rather, we must view them with a perspective that understands God as provider of all. Lives and marriages filtered through a heavenly perspective obtain a peaceful realization that what is lost on earth pales in comparison to what we gain through our relationship with God. The incorporation of this perspective in their marriage allowed Abraham and Sarah to look through the passing vale of time, beyond the senses, and to focus on God's spiritual provision for them. They simply refused to be bound by what they saw or experienced emotionally because their reliance (faith) was on God, their obedience was to God, and now we see they viewed life through God's eyes.

More Perspective—

Further evidence of the godly perspective woven into their relationship is found in Hebrews 11:11-12.

> By faith even Sarah herself received ability to conceive, even beyond the proper time of life, since she considered Him faithful who had promised. Therefore there was born even of one man, and him as good as dead at that, as many descendants AS THE STARS OF HEAVEN IN NUMBER, AND INNUMERABLE AS THE SAND WHICH IS BY THE SEASHORE.

At the age of eighty, way past her time of being able to get pregnant, Sarah conceived a child. Now the first mention of her conception, in Genesis 18:12, records that she laughed when God told her she would have children—which I would say would be a pretty typical reaction for an eighty-year-old today, also. However, in Hebrews 11, she is lauded as having a godly perspective about her conception as having come about from the One who promised. Sarah was able to see God more than the logic-based limitations. This perspective allowed her and husband Abraham the ability to receive the promise of having an innumerable number of descendants—a result unattainable apart from their perspective of God's ability above their human capacity.

Just like Abraham and Sarah's relationship, modern marriages are filled with trials that seem impossible, but the proper perspective of the One to whom we have committed our life—Jesus Christ—is what provides the strength to thrive, even in the midst of marital difficulties.

What is seen consistently in the marriage of Abraham and Sarah is the exercise of these three areas of faith, obedience and a godly perspective. For them, these three exercises produce a durable marriage that could withstand life's trials, as we have already seen. Each of these three attributes shift the result of the outcome from their hands into more capable hands. But note that faith, obedience, and godly perspective are referred to *exercises* in this chapter for a reason. They are labeled this way because they are not traits that a couple obtains by osmosis or by wishing for them. Rather, each of these three attributes is obtained by husbands and wives working hard to cultivate them on a daily basis. On the way to developing these three attributes a couple will experience their share of muscle cramps and soreness, but to achieve a relationship able to endure the pressures of marriage keep exercising. As we continue interacting with marriages of the Bible through this book we will add daily *exercises* to help cultivate *faith, obedience and godly perspective* in your marriage.

The Role Model: Faith, Obedience, Perspective

Through Abraham and Sarah, we have seen a husband and wife that model durability as they exercised faith, obedience and a godly perspective, throughout their relationship. In the early years, they exercised these attributes when they broke ties with the familiar in order to follow God. Toward the end of their marriage, they continued to exercise together as they received a son and then were willing to offer him back to God. We have also seen the times when they did not exercise these characteristics. They feared the people of Egypt while trusting God. In addition, Sarah heard God's promise of a son and laughed. Yet, both the times of exercising and not exercising their faith in the Lord work together to demonstrate the durability of a relationship with God and thus with each other.

While the particular situations may be different in your own marriage, the exercises are the same: faith, obedience, and a godly perspective comprise the model for the picture of durability we also seek to acquire The prolonged absence or inconsistency of any of these three attributes renders relationships vulnerable to being overtaken by life's challenges. On the other hand, as you respond to life with faith, obedience and a godly perspective, you will receive from God a durability that withstands both the big and mundane challenges to your marriage. Each of these three points of relationship with God comes down to a couple's consistent response to God throughout their marriage. Now that we have the model, a glimpse of the end picture of faith, obedience, and godly perspective in mind, let's encounter some other biblical couples to deepen our perspective of the balanced marriage between *Husbands, Wives, and God.*

**Think on These Things: Passages for Further Meditation and
Memorization**

- **1 Corinthians 13:4-8** Love is patient, love is kind and is not jealous;
  love does not brag and is not arrogant, does not act unbecomingly; it
  does not seek its own, is not provoked, does not take into account a
  wrong suffered, does not rejoice in unrighteousness, but rejoices with
  the truth; bears all things, believes all things, hopes all things, endures all things. Love never fails; but if there are gifts of prophecy,
  they will be done away; if there are tongues, they will cease; if there
  is knowledge, it will be done away.

- **Romans 5:19** For as through the one man's disobedience the many
  were made sinners, even so through the obedience of the One the
  many will be made righteous.

- **Galatians 3:6-9** Even so Abraham BELIEVED GOD, AND IT WAS
  RECKONED TO HIM AS RIGHTEOUSNESS. Therefore, be sure
  that it is those who are of faith who are sons of Abraham. The Scripture, foreseeing that God would justify the Gentiles by faith, preached
  the gospel beforehand to Abraham, saying, "ALL THE NATIONS
  WILL BE BLESSED IN YOU." So then those who are of faith are
  blessed with Abraham, the believer.

- **Romans 16:25-27** Now to Him who is able to establish you
  according to my gospel and the preaching of Jesus Christ, according to the revelation of the mystery which has been kept secret for
  long ages past, but now is manifested, and by the Scriptures of the
  prophets, according to the commandment of the eternal God, has
  been made known to all the nations, leading to obedience of faith;
  to the only wise God, through Jesus Christ, be the glory forever.
  Amen.

- **Romans 4:3-9** For what does the Scripture say? "ABRAHAM
  BELIEVED GOD, AND IT WAS CREDITED TO HIM AS
  RIGHTEOUSNESS." Now to the one who works, his wage is not
  credited as a favor, but as what is due. But to the one who does not
  work, but believes in Him who justifies the ungodly, his faith is

credited as righteousness, just as David also speaks of the blessing on the man to whom God credits righteousness apart from works: "BLESSED ARE THOSE WHOSE LAWLESS DEEDS HAVE BEEN FORGIVEN, AND WHOSE SINS HAVE BEEN COVERED. BLESSED IS THE MAN WHOSE SIN THE LORD WILL NOT TAKE INTO ACCOUNT." Is this blessing then on the circumcised, or on the uncircumcised also? For we say, "FAITH WAS CREDITED TO ABRAHAM AS RIGHTEOUSNESS."

- **Hebrews 11:1-3** Now faith is the assurance of things hoped for, the conviction of things not seen. For by it the men of old gained approval. By faith we understand that the worlds were prepared by the word of God, so that what is seen was not made out of things which are visible.

Husbands, Wives, God: Talking Points

1. Who, if any one, have you modeled your thoughts and actions about marriage after?

2. Does faith in God make a difference to you in your marriage? If so, how so specifically?

3. What are your perspectives, or views, on the following areas relative to marriage:

   A. Paying Bills

   B. Raising Children

   C. Roles of Men and Women in Marriage

   How are our perspectives different?

4. What characteristics from the marriage of Abraham and Sarah are relevant to our marriage?

Chapter Two

Jacob and Leah:
From Pain to Praise

Marriage Principles in This Chapter:
- Developing Godly Solutions
- Learning to Praise the Lord

*I*N THE LAST CHAPTER we looked at three defining traits of Abraham and Sarah's marriage. Now in this chapter we will look a little more closely at how one of those traits, perspectives—which shapes the overall health of a relationship.

A few years ago I had an unusual day where on the same afternoon I visited two different men, both facing their last few days. The conversations on that day with these two men provided good insight into how perspectives affect the quality of a marriage. In the context of marriage, a "perspective" is the way that a husband and wife evaluate[1] both the way they relate to each other and the quality of their marriage.

With both of these men staring into the bleak reality of their future, they openly reflected on how they had evaluated and related to their respective spouses during the years of their marriage. It seems that

---

[1] *Webster's II New Riverside Dictionary* (Boston: Houghton Mifflin, 1996) defines "evaluate" as (1) to determine the value of; (2) to examine carefully, appraise.

facing the inevitably of death brings about a clearer perspective on life and marriage, a vantage point that may have been missing in better times. I know, I know—death or the loss of a spouse is not something we like to think about. It is not my favorite topic either, especially when I think about life without my wife. But as 1 Thessalonians 4:13 reminds us regarding the death of a Christian, we have a reason to hope since our loved one is going to heaven to be with the Lord Jesus Christ. Additionally, by looking from the end of marriage backward, a couple gains insight on how to live from where they are forward.

Unhealthy Perspective, Unhealthy Marriage

As I sat with the first man, he wept openly and bitterly as he reflected on how he had treated his wife during the course of their marriage. He attributed their years of financial and emotional strain, as well as the burdens that he was leaving his wife to deal with after his death, to his stubbornness and unwillingness to listen to her during their marriage. His perspective of his wife's role in their marriage had been that her input was worthless or subordinate to his. This husband's evaluation of his wife led him to dominate his wife and to control every aspect of their relationship. His exalted appraisal of himself and low opinion of his spouse resulted in an unhealthy perspective. This unhealthy perspective kept him unwilling to accept his wife's input; instead, he disregarded her contributions to making key decisions and eventually relegated her to the sidelines of their marriage. In his final days, with time to lie in bed and reflect on their life together, he realized that his ill-founded perspectives of his role as a husband and his wife's worth had strangled the joy from their marriage.

Healthy Perspective, Healthy Marriage

Conversely, the second man was facing the same fate as the first, yet as I visited with him, he articulated a very different attitude about the inevitability of his death. As soon as I walked into the room, it was apparent that this man and his marriage had been shaped by a different assessment (perspective) of his life and marriage. This couple was singing gospel songs and hymns, clapping and laughing during those last weeks. Rejoicing over and being thankful for the good years they had shared together, they faced this most difficult time with a sense of genuine joy that enabled them to endure the breaking of their hearts. Sure, there was fear and bouts of uncertainty, but their evaluation (perspective) of the situation was that they had enjoyed a good life together and for that they were thankful to God. The husband shared with me that his approach to marriage was to always accept his wife as a gift from God, even when he did not agree with her viewpoint. He was clearly the head of their home, but his wife was highly valued, appreciated, and respected. As a result, he and his wife had built a love and friendship that grew even until his last day.

These two men held very different perspectives on their marriages. One saw marriage as something to control and that had to fit into his way of thinking. The other saw marriage as a joint venture in which both had input and which was something to enrich the relationship. He often laid aside his point of view to listen to his wife and receive her contribution. The polar opposite paths these two marriages traveled illustrates how perspectives mitigate the overall quality of a marriage. They can strangle the love out of a marriage, or they can usher love into a marriage. In spite of the circumstances that arise during the course of a marriage, the way in which a husband and wife choose to evaluate each other determines the path that the relationship will travel.

If you could fast forward to the end of your marriage, which of the two marriages above would you wish to be able to identify with? Would it be the one strangled by rigid perspectives or the one allowed to thrive by seeing the spouse as an equal? Okay, the answer may be too obvious: few if any of us would willingly choose to be in a bad marriage and suffer the misery of regret. Yet, as the ever increasing divorce rate evidences, even with the deep desire to get the most out of their relationships, many couples end up lamenting their lives together. It is a lament that is often the result of the inability to understand and effectively communicate their perspectives about life, marriage, and love, throughout the marriage. How they choose to manage their perspectives and allow them to shape their marriage is the choice between having a lifetime of marital partnership or a lifetime of marital misery. I am not suggesting that we ignore our feelings, opinions, or views in order to experience a peaceful marriage but rather, that we don't allow hardened perspectives to diminish the quality of our marriage.

As we now take the next step toward building a better marriage through building a better relationship with God, I would like to introduce you to a marriage that emphasizes the benefit of developing godly perspectives despite the conditions of the marriage. In this marriage, you can just about hear them asking a question that tough circumstances sometimes push couples to the point of asking: "Where is God in the middle of our marriage?" Yet despite the inordinate strain on their marriage, God will develop in them a perspective that enables this couple to *Praise God.* This perspective of praise is different than a shout of joy. Rather, it is a praise that requires a change of perspective—a change of scenery, if you will. It is the marriage of Jacob and Leah. Through this marriage of old, we will explore the development of a godly perspective in Leah.

The Beginnings of a Bad Marriage

In Genesis 29, we meet a woman named Leah in what I consider to be the epitome of a bad marriage. She is married to Jacob, the son of Isaac who is the son of Abraham. In the beginning of Genesis 29, Jacob had been sent out by his mother to find a wife for himself and saw a woman named Rachel that he was immediately attracted to. The Bible tells us that when Jacob first spoke with Rachel, she was so fine that he kissed her and cried. As a man, that always makes me laugh: Rachel must have been some kind of beautiful to make Jacob cry with just a kiss. After he stopped crying, Jacob was introduced to her father, Laban. Laban, who was also Jacob's uncle, had two daughters: Rachel, whom Jacob has already met and kissed, and Leah.

Rachel is described as beautiful of form and face (Gen. 29:17); however, Leah is said to be weak of eye. There are several theories as to what "weak of eye" means. To some, it means that she was severely cross-eyed; to others, it describes how unattractive she was; while some suggest it is a reference to Leah having light-colored eyes (which is the view that I hold). Regardless of how it is interpreted, the idea is that Jacob rejects Leah simply because of her physical attributes. The text does not say that she was a bad person or that her character was undesirable—simply that in some way she did not look the part. In a sense, the mention of Leah as being weak of eye heightens the degree to which she is mistreated. For whatever the meaning of the expression, it is something beyond her control that has little to do with who she is as a person. Yet because of her being weak of eye, Jacob valued or desired Rachel instead of Leah.

Based on Jacob's desire for Rachel, he and Laban enter into an agreement. The agreement was that Jacob would work for Laban for seven years, and at the end of those seven years Jacob would be married to Rachel. As Gen. 29:17 states, Jacob loved Rachel so much that the seven years felt like just a few days. At the end of the seven years Jacob asks Laban for his wife. Laban prepared the marriage feast, got his daughter Leah ready, and gave her to Jacob in marriage. Did you catch that? Laban gave his older daughter Leah, not Rachel, for whom Jacob worked seven years, and unaware of Laban's cunning ways, he married her.

The next morning, Jacob realizes that he is married to the wrong woman, literally. Upon discussing it with Laban, Jacob is basically told: too bad-so sad, you have to marry the older daughter first. Consequently, Jacob works another seven years for Rachel, so at the end of fourteen years, Jacob ends up married to *both* Leah and Rachel. Can you imagine two sisters married to the same man? Not only is he married to both sisters, but he really only wanted to be married to Rachel. The other one, Leah, is considered weak of eye and had to be married off by her father in what might be the original case of bait and switch. Quite naturally, the relationship between Jacob and Leah was terrible. As a matter of fact, the Bible says that Jacob hated Leah and loved Rachel. God saw that Leah was hated and He gave her the ability to have children, but Rachel, the one Jacob loved, was barren. Up to this point in the story, if anyone has a right to have a bad perspective about their marriage, it would be Leah.

Developing a Proper Perspective

Given the awful position that Leah was in, married to a man by means of deceit who is also married to her sister, Leah enters this marriage determined to win her husband's love by any means necessary. It appears to be her perspective that her marriage to Jacob is her source of happiness—a common and also very faulty perspective that persists even today. Another person can never be a lasting source of happiness. While it may work for a period of time, eventually your spouse will disappoint in some way because that is human nature. I tell every couple with whom I meet the same thing: "The person you married is as much a result of the fall of Adam and Eve as you are," which simply means that even though your spouse is given to complement you (discussed in full in chapter 6), your spouse has faults and flaws just like you do. While it may make for a great romantic line in a movie, in truth there is not a person on earth, including your spouse, who can complete you. Only the God who created you can truly complete you.

Jacob's perspective of Leah was not much better. His evaluation of her is that she is weak of eye and not the woman he wanted, and as a result, he hated her. So the question arises, "How can a marriage with so little to build on, and with such mutual negative perspectives of each other, have any hope of getting better?" It is a question that many couples face today. The set of circumstances may differ, but many marriages come to a point where they become hardened and controlled by their partners' evaluation of their spouse, themselves, or their relationship, based on life experiences and worldviews. When this occurs, it is difficult for them to see any hope for their marriage. Thankfully, the four distinct ways in which Leah manages her perspectives in Genesis 29:31-35 give us insight into how the perspectives we carry into, develop, and hold in our marriages can be changed by God.

> When the LORD saw that Leah was not loved, he opened her womb, but Rachel was barren. Leah became pregnant and gave birth to a son. She named him Reuben, for she said, "It is because the LORD has seen my misery. Surely my husband will love me now." She conceived again, and when she gave birth to a son she said, "Because the LORD heard that I am not loved, he gave me this one too." So she named him Simeon. Again she conceived, and when she gave birth to a son she said, "Now at last my husband will become attached to me, because I have borne him three sons." So he was named Levi. She conceived again, and when she gave birth to a son she said, "This time I will praise the LORD." So she named him Judah. Then she stopped having children.

#1 Rueben: Look at what I have done for You!

God saw that Leah was unloved (in some translations, it says she was hated) and He gave her the ability to conceive. Leah uses this gift from God to begin having children. However, Leah's motive for having a child is to change the perspective of her husband toward her. Leah names her first child, Rueben, which in Hebrew literally means, *look, a son*. By naming the child Rueben, she is in effect saying, "Hey Jacob, look at the good thing that I have done; I have given you a firstborn son, so now you have to love me." I can see her holding up the child and saying look at what I have done for you: you have to love me now. Her expectation is that because she has given Jacob a son, he should now love her. Her actions are being driven by her logic and are an attempt to gain the approval of her husband by her physical actions. Her reasoning tells her that if she gives her husband a son, then he will love her.

The point is that Leah feels she has to do something external to win Jacob's affection and to ease her internal pain. We see her "fix" through the birth of a child. While it may manifest itself differently in modern marriages, it is the same attempt to "fix" a marriage through doing something that is being reenacted in so many marriages today—that if we can get our spouse to see our worth or value based on what we do for them, then they will come to appreciate us.

#2 Simeon: Understand my pain

Apparently, Leah's first attempt was unsuccessful, so she then tries a second time. Again Leah seeks to rectify her pain by doing something external to win her husband's affection. She names her second child, Simeon, which means *to hear or understand*. This time she is saying: if I can just get him to "Hear and understand me, maybe then he will love me." Apparently, her belief is that if she can get Jacob to identify with her emotional pain, then he will become connected to her. This strategy may work temporarily, but it will not be a lasting or long-term solution. In fact, it often takes on more of the look of weakness and pity than of bringing a couple closer together. The harsh reality is that your spouse may never understand you, or they may never take the time to listen. If you have placed yourself in their hands by waiting for them to understand you, what then will that mean for your peace of mind? Will you ever be at peace? That is the situation that Leah is putting herself in. She wants Jacob to understand her heartbreak, to hear and connect with her pain in their marriage, thinking that if she can just get him to identify with her emotionally, then she will find peace. The problem is that it never happens. Jacob still did not love her.

#3 Levi: Resigned to circumstantial love

Recapping Leah's attempts at love in this awfully tough marriage, we see that she first attempted to get Jacob to see her value, and then she attempted to get him to understand how she felt. Now she has a third child, Levi. Her assumption is that Jacob must love her at this point because she has given him three sons. Like the other two children, the name sheds light on her intention. Levi means *to be attached*. With this third son, I can hear Leah saying something like this, "Look, we are too far into this. Even if you don't love me for who I am, then based on our circumstances (three children), become attached to me and love me." Her desire is that Jacob will love her because their lives have become so interwoven. Sometimes couples can grow so discouraged with their marriage that they resign themselves to toughing it out rather than trying to resolve their issues, which we see with Leah. As she evaluates their relationship, she adopts the perspective that it is just easier to stay together, even if things never get better.

At this writing (2009), we are in the throes of a global financial crisis. Unfortunately, the pressures brought on by this unprecedented economic disaster, including a rapid decrease in home values, is forcing many couples who might otherwise divorce to continue to live together solely for financial reasons. In these marriages, husbands and wives are resigned to the fact that their marriage is over but financial conditions dictate that they should stay together physically. That appears to be similar to the line of reasoning Leah is using here. She has made multiple attempts to win her husband and heal the marriage, all to no avail. So at this point she hopelessly resigns herself to the perspective that the way things are is how it will be. As she essentially says, "If you won't love me at least stay because of the three children". At this point, she rationalizes that Jacob should appreciate her and love her solely because of the circumstances of their interwoven lives.

In Leah's three attempts to win her husband's love, all of the typical methods trumpeted from the cover of many of today's magazines at the local newsstand or grocery store are utilized. This idea that a husband or wife has to do something "externally" to fix the relationship continues to keep husbands and wives wanting more and receiving less from their spouse, just as we see Leah continually putting her sense of peace in her husband's hands to no avail. It still frustrates couples today.

In fact, her first three attempts to change Jacob's perspective about her and receive his love remind me of a guy that I met on the golf course several years ago. He was a Christian ministry leader who was in the middle of a divorce. After we discovered our mutual love for the Lord, we began to talk openly about life. He shared that, throughout his marriage, his wife kept asking for more love and, in his mind that translated to material fixes, such as bigger cars and diamond rings. Ultimately, his attempts to fix the marriage from an outside-in approach led them to divorce after nearly thirty years of marriage and ministry together. It was a reminder that the longing of all our hearts is not for more stuff or techniques, but for genuine love from the heart.

When a couple attempts to heal their broken perspectives by doing "something," every action and expression of affection that they display carries with it a desperate hope that they will be valued by their spouse. It often sounds like this: "If I can just lose some weight, become more attractive, buy the right gift, make more money, etc., then he or she will love me." The reality is that just as it did not work for Leah in ancient times, it does not work in modern marriages either. The truth is that a long-term solution for the strain in a relationship is rarely, if ever, reached by "doing something." If anything, these attempts serve to intensify the pain and distance in the marriage, because as the attempts to "fix" the marriage fail to effect any change, a deeper frustration sets in. The swell of frustration eventually causes the couple to say, "I have tried and it did not work; therefore our differences must be irreconcilable." Thankfully, God's Word does provide insight on how to reconcile the differences that exist in our marriages.

#4 Judah: This Time I will Praise the Lord

Let me pose a question: "Do you desire change in your marriage so much that you are willing to adopt a different perspective?" Because eventually, that is what Leah did. After trying everything she could through her own means, she was finally ready to shed her external attempts to find peace that were centered on Jacob. Anyone can do as Leah did and adopt a negative, limited perspective that only focuses on external results. But with each of her attempts to get Jacob to pay attention to her, she was failing to pay attention to God. With each child she conceived, there was a mention of God, but she never really encounters Him. This type of casual relationship with the Lord would never have been able to generate the relationship she wanted with Jacob. In short, while trying to get her husband to change his perspective, the bigger issue was her own perspective of God.

With the conception of her fourth child, however, Leah finally exhibits the type of godly perspective that leads to an effective change, by determining that "'This time I will praise the Lord.' Therefore she named him Judah. Then she stopped bearing" (Gen. 29:35). Finally, Leah, finally! For the first time since she had married Jacob, her focus was on the Lord more than on her husband. Finally winning the love of her husband became secondary to her relationship with the Lord. Leah had now reached a point where her perspective on gaining peace wasn't dependent on her husband, but on God. As long as her peace was dependent upon her husband, something was missing. When she determined to rely on God to find her peace, she stopped bearing children. Is your perspective of happiness resting on the attitudes and actions of your spouse, or of the Lord?

That she named her fourth child Judah is interesting. Up to this point, each of Leah's children has been named in line with her perspective. With Reuben, she wanted Jacob to love her because she gave him a son. With Simeon, she wanted Jacob to hear and understand her pain. With Levi, she wanted Jacob to be attached to her because of their situation. Each child was tagged with a corresponding expectation.

By naming this child Judah, she is specifying her praise. She does not have in mind a "Hallelujah" shout or a dance or an outward expression of praise that would typically be associated with our Sunday morning church experiences. Instead, Judah has a wide range of meanings from *throw onto* (cf. Lamentations 3:53) to, *to confess* (cf. Job 40:14)[2]. Therefore, an accurate understanding of what Leah is saying in this fourth attempt is, "This time, I will confess my pain to the Lord," or said another way, "This time, I will throw my pain onto the Lord." Wow! This is so much different than the way she has previously handled the dysfunction of her marriage.

Her perspective to this point had been that the problem was with Jacob—he did not love her—and the solution rested on her shoulders. In reality, the problem was in her searching for acceptance from her spouse instead of from God. Likewise, the solution was to refocus on God rather than her husband. By naming her fourth child Judah, she was making a humble proclamation of the truth: she couldn't make Jacob love her. This time, she determined to make a step toward God and thus take the stress off of the marriage. This time, she is aligning herself with God and gaining the understanding that we cannot change our spouse or even ourselves without God. Her confession is that the way out of a strained marriage is through a changed perspective and a deeper relationship with God, not through the plans we can devise.

When I was a young boy, my father would play this game with my sister and me where he would push down on our shoulders and say in the real crazy deep voice, "Does it feel like the weight of the world is on your shoulders?" and I would push as hard as I could with my little legs to stand up. Then he would take his hands off my shoulders and I would go flying up in the air, and we would crack up laughing. In a very real sense, this is what happened with Leah. For however many years Leah and Jacob have been married, she has been carrying the

---

[2] Francis Brown with cooperation from S. R. Driver and Charles A. Briggs, *The Brown-Driver Briggs Hebrew and English Lexicon: With an Appendix Containing the Biblical Aramaic* (Massachusetts: Hendrickson Publishers, Inc. – Reprinted from the 1906 edition originally published by Houghton, Mifflin and Company, 7th Printing 2003), page 392.

weight of the world on her shoulders, trying to fix their marriage. But by throwing her pain onto the Lord and taking it off of her own shoulders, she removed that big burden of stress and the hurt of being hated by her husband. Her confession lightened her load.

The real blessing here is that we, too, are able to unburden, or at least greatly reduce, the stressors that weigh down our emotions, our desires, and our passions for each other. The same way that Leah took the weight off her marriage by throwing her situation onto the Lord is available today. I am convinced that many of the burdens on marriages today we were neither intended or built to handle. It is the kind of weight that leaves couples tired, burned out, and ready to give up. But notice how much stress she takes off of herself when she throws her stress onto the Lord, as verse 35 says, "Then she stopped bearing."[3] The multiple attempts to fix her marriage by herself only resulted in the same disappointing outcome, until she changed her relationship with God. We simply cannot employ techniques to try to maintain spiritual balance in relationships. Until we learn to throw our problems off of us and onto the Lord, marriages will be unduly burdened.

Changed Perspective, Changed Relationship

Leah's changed perspective of relationship with God over external fixes, led to a changed relationship with God. It appears that there were at least two positive changes resulting from Leah's praise. I want to be careful not to over-speculate about what changes actually occurred in Jacob and Leah's marriage. I was not there, and the Bible does not explicitly say that their marriage got better, but it appears that somewhere along the line the marriage between Jacob and Leah improved. First, in Genesis 49:31, it states that Leah was buried with Jacob and the rest of the family, and specifically, with Abraham, Sarah, Isaac, and Rebekah. On the other hand, Rachel, for whom Jacob previously expressed such deep love, was buried apart from the family (cf. Gen.

---

[3] Unfortunately, Leah's sense of peace is temporary; she would eventually return to having more children and continuing to compete with her sister, Rachel.

35:19-20; 48:7). What is interesting is that Jacob's beloved Rachel was buried apart from the family and yet he buried the one whom he initially hated with him and in the esteemed company of his parents and grandparents.

The second significant change as a result of Leah's throwing her heartache onto the Lord was that she gained acceptance into God's family. In Matthew 1:2, where the lineage of Jesus is given, Judah is the only son of Jacob's twelve sons mentioned by name: "Jacob the father of Judah and his brothers." Then in Matthew 1:3, the lineage of Jesus continues through Judah's son Perez. The connection between Leah's son, Judah, and the lineage of Jesus is further illustrated in Hebrews 7:14: "For it is evident that our Lord was descended from Judah..." and again, in Revelation 5:5, Jesus is referred to as the Lion of the Tribe of Judah. Leah's praise was a confession of weakness to God, not just lip service, and from it comes entrance into the family of God. Her husband did not initially want her in his family but God used her changed perspective to incorporate her into God's family.

Learn to adopt this perspective of *Praising God* in your marriage, meaning, confessing to God where there is hurt, pain, joy, and desire—whatever the case may be. In today's divorce-prone environment, where 35% of Christian marriages as well of 35% of non-Christian marriages end in divorce,[4] it would have been acceptable for Leah to divorce her husband. Instead, she changed her perspective, praised God and found peace.

Leah could have chosen to evaluate her marriage through the same rigid perspective that she began with. She could have seen it as helpless, and kept seeking to win her husband through fruitless external means, but she adopted a changed perspective through a changed relationship with God.

---

[4] The Barna Group, "Born-Again Christians Just as Likely to Divorce as are Non-Christians," at http://www.barna.org/barna-update/article/5-barna-update/194-born-again-christians-just-as-likely-to-divorce-as-are-non-christians (accessed August 18, 2009).

How to throw "It" on the Lord

So how do we throw our problems onto the Lord, as Leah did? Well, the very meaning of the name Judah provides a hint. As mentioned earlier, Judah means to confess or throw onto. So then, in the midst of difficult conditions that are sometimes present in our marriage, we must throw our hurt, pain, frustration, disappointment, and so forth onto God in prayer.

1.   Confess for clarity. Admit to God through prayer those areas where you have a faulty perspective. This is a personal confession that really has little to do with the behavior of your spouse. Our confession to the Lord may or may not change our spouse's behavior or the conditions in our marriages. What confession does is to give the wounded person or persons a godly perspective to deal with their reality.

By confessing our weaknesses, we are able to see the strength of God, as He changes our perspective on our feelings, our spouse, and our marriage. I can attest personally that when I confess where I am weak and making a mess of my marriage because of my faulty perspectives, even more areas of fault, responsibility, and weakness than I originally understood come into focus. By understanding the various points where my perspective is flawed, I get a clear picture of what needs to change. In the case of Leah, as long as she relied on her plans, there was no change. However, when she took her pain and disappointments and threw them onto the Lord, she was able to see her poor perspective and to embrace a new perspective, which then led to a new relationship with God and her spouse.

2.   Make a list of the areas that are identified as weaknesses and begin to pray about them. Now that there is some clarity as to where your evaluation of the marriage (a.k.a., your perspective) is hindering the relationship, make a list of these areas. From this list begin to pray to God for wisdom that he will direct you and your spouse in these areas of your relationship. This is throwing "it" on the Lord (See Chapter 5 for more about prayer).

I pray for each individual and couple reading this book that this takes hold in your marriage, because it provides a level of freedom in a relationship that is simply priceless. It reminds me of the words of the Apostle Paul in Galatians 5:1, when he talks about the reason that Christ came to set us free. He explains, "It was for freedom that Christ set us free; therefore keep standing firm and do not be subject again to a yoke of slavery." Allow God to free you from perspectives that are hindering your marriage from progressing in the way that God intended when He joined the two of you together.

Up to this point, we have been looking at "throwing it" on the Lord from an individual standpoint. However, it becomes even more powerful when a husband and wife can join together and confess areas of weakness. There may be areas that you *and* your spouse agree are weak points in your marriage. Begin to confess these areas to the Lord together. For example, I am a new father; I have had to confess to God that there are some areas of fatherhood, such as disciplining our child, that just scare me and about which I have no idea what to do. As a couple, my wife and I have to confess that we are learning as we go and we have no clue what we are doing in raising our son. This in no way makes me weak as a husband, head of household, or father. In fact, I believe it makes me stronger when I confess to God that I am weak without Him. When couples can openly confess their flaws to God and to each other, it creates a humility that the Lord can work with, which in turn fortifies the marriage bond between the Husband, Wife and God.

On a consistent basis, allow God to enter into your relationship as you "throw it on the Lord". Can you and your spouse commit to one day a week, as a starting point, to make time, in prayer, to throw areas of your marriage that you need help with onto God? Have fun with it, identify and address specific areas where your relationship needs divine help – throw it on the Lord. As you and your spouse begin to see your areas of growth and confess them to the Lord, He will begin to provide wisdom to strengthen your marriage.

Relating Jacob and Leah to Your Marriage

In this chapter we looked at three marriages—those of the two men facing the last days of their life, and then of Leah. As I once again think on those two men that shared their reflections of their marriage while on their deathbeds, it becomes clear that the man who had the admittedly unhealthy perspective failed to clearly see God in his evaluation of life and marriage, until it was too late. The ability to evaluate life with a godly perspective is available to all who praise the Lord by confessing faulty earthly perspectives and then throwing them on the Lord in prayer. Don't wait until the end of your marriage to praise the Lord. Let me summarize this chapter this way: Leah was in the epitome of a bad marriage, about as bad as it can get. She went through numerous attempts to "right" the relationship on her own, eventually removing the stress from her own shoulders and putting it onto the Lord. Leah's struggle brings to mind a final scripture worth thinking about from Psalm 150:6, "Let everything that has breath praise the Lord. Praise the Lord!" Determine in your own marriage, "This time we will Praise the Lord!"

Think on These Things: Passages for Further Meditation and Memorization

- **Isaiah 38:18** Death cannot Praise You.

- **Psalm 103:1-2** Bless the Lord, O my soul, And all that is within me, bless His holy name. Bless the Lord, O my soul, And forget none of His benefits;

- **Psalm 106:1** Praise the Lord! Oh give thanks to the Lord, for He is good; For His lovingkindness is everlasting

- **Matthew 9:20-22** And a woman who had been suffering from a hemorrhage for twelve years, came up behind Him and touched the fringe of His cloak: for she was saying to herself, "If I only touch His garment, I will get well." But Jesus turning and seeing her said, "Daughter take courage; your faith has made you well." At once the woman was made well.

- **Hebrews 13:4-5** Marriage is to be held in honor among all, and the marriage bed is to be undefiled; for fornicators and adulterers God will judge. Make sure that your character is free from the love of money, being content with what you have; for He Himself has said, "I WILL NEVER DESERT YOU, NOR WILL I EVER FORSAKE YOU,"

- **Hebrews 13:15-16** Through Him then, let us continually offer up a sacrifice of praise to God, that is, the fruit of lips that give thanks to His name. And do not neglect doing good and sharing, for with such sacrifices God is pleased.

Husbands, Wives, God: Talking Points

1. Is Leah's idea of praising God different from how you have
    traditionally thought of praising God?

2. What is one area of our marriage that we need to "throw onto"
    God?

3. Do you identify with any of those first three ways in which Leah
    tried to reach her husband?

4. Do you think God's fix for our marriage is more effective than our
    fix, how so?

5. What is your perspective of a husband/wife in marriage? In what
    ways do I fit/not fit this perspective?

Chapter Three

Job and Mrs. Job:
In God We Trust

Marriage Principles in This Chapter:
- Building Relationship of Trust Between Husbands, Wives and God
- Trusting in God to sustain a marriage

*T*HE BOOK OF JOB is one of the most beloved books of the Bible, recognized for the timeless question it poses and then answers, "Why do the righteous suffer?" Job is the oft-told narrative of an upright and righteous man's wrestling to hold onto his faith through the devastating loss of his wealth, health, and ten children. However, this poignantly relevant story chronicles more than the suffering of its namesake, for accompanying Job on his journey through his valley of the shadow of death is his wife.

As was the case with Job and his wife, hard times are inevitable in marriage and every couple will face their share of tenuous times at more than one point in their marriage. The hardships of Job and his wife, however, reach extremes that I pray no one reading this book ever endures. Yet a closer look at how this biblical couple handles severe adversity reveals the powerful role that trust plays in a marriage. What amazes me about this story is that it is not trust in each other, but an unshakable trust in God that preserves this marriage through trials that would grind most people to powder.

Meet Job

There was a man in the land of Uz whose name was Job; and that man was blameless, upright, fearing God and turning away from evil.

Seven sons and three daughters were born to him. His possessions also were 7,000 sheep, 3,000 camels, 500 yoke of oxen, 500 female donkeys, and very many servants; and that man was the greatest of all the men of the east. His sons used to go and hold a feast in the house of each one on his day, and they would send and invite their three sisters to eat and drink with them. When the days of feasting had completed their cycle, Job would send and consecrate them, rising up early in the morning and offering burnt offerings according to the number of them all; for Job said, "Perhaps my sons have sinned and cursed God in their hearts. "Thus Job did continually. (Job 1:1-5)

In the opening five verses of the book of Job, he is introduced as an upright man of high moral character. He was the father of ten children—seven sons and three daughters—and a wealthy man with exceptional financial security through an abundance of livestock, land, houses, and servants. Even more than all of his material wealth, he was a man of deep and abiding spiritual conviction, which led him to rise early in the morning to pray, consecrate, and make sacrifices for his children.

Job's relationship with God was not a momentary or circumstance-driven trust, but a thread that was woven into and throughout every aspect of his life. As a result of his trust relationship with God, he was seen as the greatest man of the east to all that came in contact with him (cf. Job, ch. 29).

However, neither his financial stature and honor among people, nor his relationship with God, exempted him from life's difficulties. In fact, as the Bible states, there was a day when Satan was looking for someone to devour and God proffers Job for Satan to afflict with hardship. Because of the character and quality of life that Job lived, God permitted Satan access to Job. It was a demonstration of God's trust in Job that he could handle whatever was sent his way. So then, into this rather enviable life intrude some pretty extreme trials, designed by Satan but allowed under the watchful eye of a sovereign God. In the span of a few short hours, Job loses everything he owns: his homes, servants, financial security, honor, his good health, and probably most painfully, his ten children. Look at how the Bible captures Job's day of utter calamity:

Now there was a day when the sons of God came to present themselves before the LORD, and Satan also came among them. The LORD said to Satan, "From where do you come?" Then Satan answered the LORD and said, "From roaming about on the earth and walking around on it." The LORD said to Satan, "Have you considered My servant Job? For there is no one like him on the earth, a blameless and upright man, fearing God and turning away from evil." Then Satan answered the LORD, "Does Job fear God for nothing? "Have You not made a hedge about him and his house and all that he has, on every side? You have blessed the work of his hands, and his possessions have increased in the land. "But put forth Your hand now and touch all that he has; he will surely curse You to Your face." Then the LORD said to Satan, "Behold, all that he has is in your power, only do not put forth your hand on him." So Satan departed from the presence of the LORD. Now on the day when his sons and his daughters were eating and drinking wine in their oldest brother's house, a messenger came to Job and said, "The oxen were plowing and the donkeys feeding beside them, and the Sabeans attacked and took them. They also slew the servants with the edge of the sword, and I alone have escaped to tell you." While he was still speaking, another also came and said, "The fire of God fell from heaven and burned up the sheep and the servants and consumed them, and I alone have escaped to tell you." While he was still speaking, another also came and said, "The Chaldeans formed three bands and made a raid on the camels and took them and slew the servants with the edge of the sword, and I alone have escaped to tell you." While he was still speaking, another also came and said, "Your sons and your daughters were eating and drinking wine in their oldest brother's house, and behold, a great wind came from across the wilderness and struck the four corners of the house, and it fell on the young people and they died, and I alone have escaped to tell you." Then Job arose and tore his robe and shaved his head, and he fell to the ground and worshiped. (Job 1:6-20)

Here is a man that has lost everything that most would consider their source of well being and importance in life. Everything that his success and honor were measured by in the first five verses of the chapter, have now been removed from his life. I can be honest with myself and say that if I were Job I would need some serious therapy at this point. The reality is that, try as we might, most of us have a real struggle to not be tied to our "stuff." The things we posses, earn, drive, our relationships, the positions we hold, etc.—all of it has a way of being equated with our sanity, esteem, and overall sense of worth.

I often think of those who lost all that they owned and were stranded for days in the wake of Hurricane Katrina. Or the thousands of Midwesterners in the spring and early summer floods of 2008. These were humble people whose homes and possessions were lifted from their foundations and swept down the streets where they had once walked hand in hand. Reflecting on the accounts and images of great loss, I often wonder how I would handle such situations. The spiritual answer is pretty clear; the tried and true clichés of the church are always available. But the truth is that there are also certain realities that are tethered to circumstances and presented before us that challenge our spiritual equilibrium and purpose in life. Realizing this makes Job stand out even more as a true "servant" of God. For in the face of losing every material possession, and then burying seven sons and three daughters, Job's first response to this terrible news is to fall to the ground and worship (v. 20). Then in verses 21 and 22, "He said, 'Naked I came from my mother's womb, And naked I shall return there. The LORD gave and the LORD has taken away. Blessed be the name of the LORD.' Through all this, Job did not sin nor did he blame God." Wow! With all that Job lost, the one thing that couldn't be taken was his trust in God.

Satan's Estimation

Behind the scenes of Job's tragic situation are two conversations between Satan and God. The first is found in Job 1:6-8, the passage used above. During that conversation, Satan is looking for someone to destroy and God demonstrates His trust in Job by saying, "Have you considered My servant Job? For there is no one like him on the earth, a blameless and upright man, fearing God and turning away from evil"

(1:8). In this conversation Satan estimates that if he could be allowed to mess with Job's material wealth, then he would turn from God. In their second conversation, Satan asks God for permission to compromise Job's health:

> Satan answered the LORD and said, "Skin for skin! Yes, all that a man has he will give for his life. However, put forth Your hand now, and touch his bone and his flesh; he will curse You to Your face." So the LORD said to Satan, "Behold, he is in your power, only spare his life." Then Satan went out from the presence of the LORD and smote Job with sore boils from the sole of his foot to the crown of his head. And he took a potsherd to scrape himself while he was sitting among the ashes. (Job 2:4-8)

These two conversations between God and Satan provide valuable insight into the Devil's estimation of people. He believes that if he is allowed to touch Job's "things" and his health, then he can cause Job to curse God and thus destroy the relationship between Job and God (cf. Job 1:11 and 2:4). It is my belief that Satan continues to view and come at people in the same manner today. He still believes that if he can just mess with the things you possess or just cause a few things to go wrong in your marriage, or if he could just cause a few trials and make things uncomfortable, then he can derail your relationship with God.

I have never run the numbers, but a considerable percentage of the couples that I have encountered through biblical or pastoral counseling can trace their marital problems back to a change in their relationship with God. At some point, a tough situation arose in their marriage, causing the trust in God of one or both to waver momentarily. Soon after, the pressure cracks began to form and it was not long until their marriage began crumbling beneath the strain—and soon, they are seeking a divorce. Yet there have also been those who, when they were able to regain a balanced relationship with God, have seen the marriage improve. So these first two chapters of Job remind us that since the early days of human existence Satan's plan has been to disrupt humankind's relationship with God through material and/or physical distress. In spite of the estimation that Satan has of people, Job demonstrates that it is possible, even in the worst of situations, to maintain your relationship with God. For in the end, the biblical report of Job in the loss of everything he owned was that "Through all this Job did not sin nor did he blame God" (Job 1:22), and again when he was ravaged with pus-filled boils from head to toe, "In all this Job did not sin with his lips" (2:10).

Meet Mrs. Job—Job's Better Half?

Clearly, Job is the main character of the book of Job, leaving the details about his wife somewhat threadbare. However, just the mere mention of a wife, as brief as it is, changes everything about this story. It is often taught and believed that Job's wife was killed in the second chapter of the book, but since the Bible does not specifically say that, I would disagree. Of the four reports that Job's servants give explaining what he lost, and breaking the news of the deaths of his servants and children, his wife is never mentioned as a casualty. In addition, she is alive and talking to Job in chapter 2 after the reports of Job's losses, the death of his servants, and after he is afflicted with agonizing boils from head to toe. Then in chapter 19, as Job recounts all the pain he has experienced, he notes that, "My breath is offensive to my wife" (19:17), indicating Mrs. Job is still alive, even that late in the story.

That being the case, it is reasonable to conclude that whatever Job went through, he went through as a married man, and that his wife endured his loss and pain with him. So rather than looking at all that Job suffered as if he were a single man, it really should be said that *they* lost their source of income, their houses, their honor, their wealth, and their ten children, for surely his wife also shared in these pains. Although they experienced similar hurts and losses, unfortunately, their reactions were very different.

Husbands, Wives, God: A Matter of Trust

Let's look deeper into how the three parties of this three-way trust relationship—Job, Mrs. Job, and God—demonstrate that trust. For his part, God has demonstrated His trust in Job, in that he allowed Satan to afflict him (cf. 1:8 and 2:6). It is worth our time to meditate deeply about the solemn reality that if God treats Job this way, what does it say about some of the trials that you and I endure? When my marriage goes through a strenuous time, I find a quiet place and ask myself this question, "Can God trust me to maintain my relationship with Him in the face of whatever these challenges may be?" In God's actions toward Job, we see the kind of mutual trust that is available to our marriages. God trusts Job; now let's see how Job and his wife trust God in return.

Job Trusts Himself and Their Situation to God

Although Job and his wife share in the same painful losses (with the exception of his sickness), their reactions are on opposite ends of the spectrum. Job exercises his faith and wrestles with his pain without sinning against God. Job's response to their situation focuses on the character and sovereignty of God. Look at Job's initial response, "Naked I came from my mother's womb, And naked I shall return there. The LORD gave and the LORD has taken away. Blessed be the name of the LORD" (Job 1:21). After making such a bold and noble statement of trust, he continues to experience "unsparing pain" (cf. 6:10) and uncertainty for the remaining thirty-or-so chapters of the book of Job. Even in his pain and bouts of uncertainty about what God is doing in his life, he continues to trust himself and his situation to God as he makes incredible statements, such as:

> "As for me, I know that my Redeemer lives, And at the last He will take His stand on the earth. Even after my skin is destroyed, Yet from my flesh I shall see God." (Job 19:25-26)

> "Though He slay me, I will hope in Him: Nevertheless I will argue my ways before Him." (Job 13:15)

> "If a man dies, will he live again? All the days of my struggle I will wait Until my change comes." (Job 14:14)

> "But He knows the way I take; When He has tried me, I shall come forth as gold." (Job 23:10)

Job did all the right things in his life; he was blameless, upright, feared God, turned from evil, and sacrificed for his children,[5] yet here he is, broke, sick, and suffering. To most people, Job's turn of events would seem unfair, but he looks beyond the circumstances and trusts both his material and physical wellbeing to God. In the good times when all was well, and also in the rough times of his life, he just kept trusting. In the same way, in whatever we identify as a tough situation, we too have the ability to keep trusting God.

Mrs. Job's Trusts Herself and Their Situation to Herself

Way on the opposite end of the spectrum of Job's response is the response of his wife. Her losses pretty much mirror her husband's, yet she is simply not able to move past the pain of what has transpired. The pain of losing their material possessions, their financial stability, and perhaps most painfully, their ten children, was more than she could handle. She became stuck in the details of what had transpired and so turns from both God and Job.[6] In Job 2:9, she responds this way: "Are you still holding on to your integrity? Curse God and die!" That's not quite the supportive response we would expect from our spouse in a time of mutual trial. She has effectively placed herself on a deserted island apart from both God and her husband. Her pain is blocking her from seeing beyond herself; all she can see is *her* pain. In more modern language she is saying, "I cannot take any more pain; enough is enough, I want a divorce." It appears that her sense of security and trust was tied up in the "things" they lost. And the reality is that life's circumstances can pressure us into trusting ourselves instead of God.

Before we dismiss Mrs. Job's decision as totally irrational, let me raise a caution flag. When I teach about Job and Mrs. Job, I ask how many people would respond like Job and how many would respond like

---

[5] I find it interesting that he sacrifices "for his children" but not for his wife.

[6] Questions sometimes arise about the quality of relationship that Job's wife had with God prior to these events. The best I can determine, it can only be speculated what her relationship with God was. My assumption, based on Job's lifestyle, is that she at least knew about God, but how well, I don't know.

Mrs. Job. More than I initially would have expected state they would respond much the same way that Mrs. Job did. I would estimate that about one-third say they would undoubtedly respond like Job, another third say they would respond like Mrs. Job, and the other third is uncertain, but say that their response would depend on the situation. In a very real sense, the contemporary divorce rate bears out that Mrs. Job is not alone in her response. We have to be honest and admit that for most of us circumstances arise which, if not dealt with, could bring us to a point of saying "Enough is enough, I can't take it anymore." She experienced a cruel set of circumstances: loss of financial security, house, life savings, and her ten children—that surely must have felt unbearable and provided a perfectly acceptable excuse, by our society's standards today, for leaving the relationship. Surely few people would fault her for being overcome with grief and thus finding it difficult to trust in God. I mean, why would God do this to her? Why did he allow this to happen? Mrs. Job might well be vindicated in her response if not for the fact that her husband Job experienced every bit and even more than his wife did, yet never lost his relationship of trust in God. He gives us hope, beyond our human strength or understanding, that there is a way of getting through our emotional and physical pain thresholds and hanging on to the hand of God.

The Purpose of the Trial

For Job, the trials were never about the material things he had lost; those were just the outward circumstances. But through the process of loss and pain, he came to a deeper understanding of who God was. In chapters 38–41, God asks Job a series of rhetorical questions that demonstrate God's wisdom and sovereignty in all of life's circumstances. Although it all seemed so unfair to Job's wife, the purpose of the entire set of trials they experienced was for Job to get to the point of saying this about God:

> I know that You can do all things, And that no purpose of Yours can be thwarted....I have heard of You by the hearing of the ear; But now my eye sees You; Therefore I retract, And I repent in dust and ashes. (Job 42:2, 5-6)

In other words, the deeper insight Job gained outweighed his losses as he came to realize three things:

1. God can do all things.
2. God's purpose cannot be thwarted.
3. God is sovereign.

Up to this point in his life, Job had experienced God in some limited sense, but now he had seen it and could internalize God's goodness for himself. Therefore, he would turn from his shallow view of God and live in a new way for God. In the same way, every trial that you face in your marriage, whether great or small, has a purpose to it. Ultimately, regardless of how deep the strain a marriage faces, the purpose is to deepen your view of God, but only if we keep on trusting God.

> After Job had prayed for his friends, the LORD made him prosperous again and gave him twice as much as he had before. All his brothers and sisters and everyone who had known him before came and ate with him in his house. They comforted and consoled him over all the trouble the LORD had brought upon him, and each one gave him a piece of silver and a gold ring. The LORD blessed the latter part of Job's life more than the first. He had fourteen thousand sheep, six thousand camels, a thousand yoke of oxen and a thousand donkeys. And he also had seven sons and three daughters. (Job 42:10-13)

Now that Job has gained the insight that God wanted him to have, his entire fortune is restored, twofold. Included in this restoration, he and his wife once again had more children: seven sons and three daughters. Although Job's wife initially was unable to see God at work, turned her back, and became consumed with her pain, she is now blessed because of her husband's continued trust in God. I can only wonder if we were able to speak to her today, what lessons she would say she learned from all of this.

As I see it, the lesson for us in the context of marriage is that every day of a couple's marital journey, there are opportunities to respond in trust to both the small and big things of life. Job and his wife remind us that Satan and, it is fair to say, the world around us, estimates that it can create a set of circumstances that will cause marriages to move away from God. On the other hand, God allows tough situations to arise in marriage to demonstrate his trust in us.

Will you then continue to trust Him? There will be trying times when your marriage will become severely strained, but keep on trusting God to restore your relationship. God's thoughts and ways are higher than ours (Isa. 55:8), but keep trusting the Righteous Judge, the Shepherd and Guardian of your soul. Trust.

How to trust God? How to trust your spouse?

Finally, let's look at three attributes of trust that Job modeled. Collectively, they make up the acronym T-A-G. Allow these three attributes to shape your interaction with your spouse:

> **T - Trust** yourself to God. By trusting yourself to God more than to your spouse, you will gain a sense of balance in the highs and lows of marriage. "As for me, I know that my Redeemer lives, And at the last He will take His stand on the earth" (Job 19:25).

> **A - Adversity** is an expected part of life. Adversity will come into every marriage, at some point, to some degree. See adversity as a part of God's sovereign plan instead of as something that will destroy your marriage. "Shall we indeed accept good from God and not accept adversity?" (Job 2:9).

> **G - God** is the provider of all that we have. We own nothing in this world. Everything that is in this world was provided by God, even our children, our spouses, and our material possessions. When we come to the end of our lives, we will not be able to take anything gained on earth with us. As it is often said, you never see a U-Haul hitched to a hearse. Do not love "things" more than either God or your spouse. "The LORD gave and the LORD has taken away" (Job 1:21).

Think on These Things: Passages for Further Meditation and Memorization

- **1 Peter 2:21-25** (key passage) For you have been called for this purpose, since Christ also suffered for you, leaving you an example for you to follow in His steps, WHO COMMITTED NO SIN, NOR WAS ANY DECEIT FOUND IN HIS MOUTH; and while being reviled, He did not revile in return; while suffering, He uttered no threats, but kept entrusting Himself to Him who judges righteously; and He Himself bore our sins in His body on the cross, so that we might die to sin and live to righteousness; for by His wounds you were healed. For you were continually straying like sheep, but now you have returned to the Shepherd and Guardian of your souls.

- **1 Peter 3:1-6 (Wives)** In the same way, you wives, be submissive to your own husbands so that even if any of them are disobedient to the word, they may be won without a word by the behavior of their wives, as they observe your chaste and respectful behavior. Your adornment must not be merely external—braiding the hair, and wearing gold jewelry, or putting on dresses; but let it be the hidden person of the heart, with the imperishable quality of a gentle and quiet spirit, which is precious in the sight of God. For in this way in former times the holy women also, who hoped in God, used to adorn themselves, being submissive to their own husbands; just as Sarah obeyed Abraham, calling him lord, and you have become her children if you do what is right without being frightened by any fear.

- **1 Peter 3:7-8 (Husbands)** You husbands in the same way, live with your wives in an understanding way, as with someone weaker, since she is a woman; and show her honor as a fellow heir of the grace of life, so that your prayers will not be hindered. To sum up, all of you be harmonious, sympathetic, brotherly, kindhearted, and humble in spirit;

- **1 Peter 3:9 (Husbands and Wives)** not returning evil for evil or insult for insult, but giving a blessing instead; for you were called for the very purpose that you might inherit a blessing.

- **James 5:11** We count those blessed who endured. You have heard of the endurance of Job and have seen the outcome of the Lord's dealings, that the Lord is full of compassion and is merciful.

- **Isaiah 55:8** "For My thoughts are not your thoughts, Nor are your ways My ways," declares the LORD.

- **Ephesians 6:10-12** Finally, be strong in the Lord and in the strength of His might. Put on the full armor of God, so that you will be able to stand firm against the schemes of the devil. For our struggle is not against flesh and blood, but against the rulers, against the powers, against the world forces of this darkness, against the spiritual forces of wickedness in the heavenly places.

- **Romans 6:12-14** Therefore do not let sin reign in your mortal body so that you obey its lusts, and do not go on presenting the members of your body to sin as instruments of unrighteousness; but present yourselves to God as those alive from the dead, and your members as instruments of righteousness to God. For sin shall not be master over you, for you are not under law but under grace.

- **1 Corinthians 13:4-7** Love is patient, love is kind and is not jealous; love does not brag and is not arrogant, does not act unbecomingly; it does not seek its own, is not provoked, does not take into account a wrong suffered, does not rejoice in unrighteousness, but rejoices with the truth; bears all things, believes all things, hopes all things, endures all things.

Husbands, Wives, God: Talking Points

1. How would the outcome of Job's life been different if his trust (reliance) had been in his wife?

2. How would the outcome have been different if Job's wife had trusted in God?

3. If we experienced similar circumstances, who would you respond like, Job or Mrs. Job?

4. What has prevented us from trusting God in our relationship?

5. What makes trusting God difficult for you?

6. What has made me difficult to trust?

Chapter Four

Manoah, His Wife, And The Angel of the Lord: Let's Talk

Marriage Principles in This Chapter:
- Three Way Communication: Husband, Wife, God
- Building God-Centered Communication
- Lord, Teach Us What to Do

*R*ECENTLY I WAS DRIVING the family back from North Carolina to Maryland and we came up on a stretch of highway that was under construction. A half-mile or so before the construction began, there was a roadside construction sign that read "New Traffic Pattern Ahead." It is funny how the most routine events can arrest our attention and become enlightening. Many times, I have come upon similar construction signs along the road-side; however, this one seemed to really jump out at me. Obviously, the purpose of the sign was to alert drivers that what they had come to expect while traveling this stretch of highway was about to change. Drivers may have been used to the highway turning left or right, but now the warning was that the familiar pattern had been changed. Maybe the pace or thickness of the traffic would be changing, whatever it was, the road construction would result in a changed pattern.

Likewise, you may be accustomed to arguments, miscommunication, and strained communication. In this chapter, we will meet a couple that has a pattern of communication that may be different from how you and your spouse presently communicate. Regardless of what you have become accustomed to, let me erect a sign on the road-side of your marriage, and it reads "Caution: New Communication Pattern Ahead." In this chapter, God's Word will provide a new and fresh way for husbands and wives to communicate with each other. Too often, as marriages move along throughout the years, negative communication patterns and routines become so engrained in the fabric of that relationship that their negative effects become imperceptible to the couple. After a while, what may have been painful in the past becomes tolerated and seen as "just the way it is." This new pattern, however, is one that enables couples to express themselves with each other and effectively exchange feelings, expressions, information, or love. In this chapter, God's Word will place the communication patterns of husbands and wives under construction and the result will be a new communication pattern for marriages.

In the context of marriage, effective communication is the "ability to give and/or exchange thoughts, opinions, information or feelings either verbally or non-verbally in a clear, relatable, and understandable ways."[7] Most couples that I come in contact with would want the interaction with their spouse to be defined this way on a consistent basis. However, for most couples, the ability to give or exchange verbally or non-verbally with their spouse in an understandable way persistently proves to be especially challenging. Instead of a consistent smooth flowing river of communication where feelings, ideas, and joy are shared, the communication relationship is more like trying to sail through a logjam. Just as a bad stretch of highway can be reconstructed to provide more suitable driving conditions, a relationship can be reconstructed to provide more effective communication.

Unfortunately, the effects of poor communication (either verbal or non-verbal) cannot be compartmentalized to just one or two areas of life together; rather, they eat away at the quality of the overall relationship—a reality which elevates the need for couples to be able to communicate effectively. In fact, I cannot think of any type of problem that arises in marriage that does not in some way relate to communication. Either the lack of effective communication is the root of the problem, or the exercise of effective communication will pave the road

---

[7] "communication," *The Oxford American Desk Dictionary and Thesaurus,* 2nd ed. (2002)

to restoring the relationship. In either case, everything in a relationship centers around how a couple communicates.

Husbands, Wives, God: Talk to Me

The typical communication pattern between husbands and wives can be characterized as a back and forth lobbing of words, feelings, opinions, or expressions. One speaks, the other responds—back and forth, back and forth, she speaks, he speaks, each time lobbing words at one another, sometimes resulting in harmony, but more often leading to points of miscommunication. It is much like watching a good tennis match. One serves, the other returns, and back and forth they go until someone wins the point.

While the goal of a tennis match is to win as many points as possible, collecting points in the communication between you and your spouse only leads to division and strain on the marriage. Rather than communicating from opposite sides of the net, husbands and wives should work toward a pattern of communication that puts them on the same side of the net. It is a pattern that reaches beyond the back and forth tennis-talk to effective communication among the Husband, the Wife, and God. In the book of Judges, there is a marriage between Samson's parents—Manoah and his wife—that demonstrates what this healthy communication pattern looks like.

Introducing Manoah and His Wife: Judges 13:1-5

In Judges 13, we meet Manoah and his wife. There is not a whole lot of background information given about this couple, but we do know that Manoah is of the tribe of Dan and his wife is unable to have children.

> Then the angel of the LORD appeared to the woman and said to her, "Behold now, you are barren and have borne no children, but you shall conceive and give birth to a son. Now therefore, be careful not to drink wine or strong drink, nor eat any unclean thing. For behold, you shall conceive and give birth to a son, and no razor shall come upon his head, for the boy shall

be a Nazirite to God from the womb; and he shall begin to deliver Israel from the hands of the Philistines." (Judges 13:3-5)

The Bible tells us that one day the Angel of the Lord appears to
Manoah's wife. The Angel makes a promise to her, with very explicit
directions about what she and Manoah are to do in regard to her
barrenness, and the child that He will give her. (See Appendix A for a
more complete discussion of the identity of the Angel of the Lord.)

Hearing from God

Many couple's spend an exorbitant amount of time and energy
trying to master external communication methods and techniques by
cramming pre-scripted rules of communication into their marriage.
However, the real fix to communication strains comes from learning
to hear from God about the issues, concerns, and stresses of marriage
so that lasting gains are experienced. This is what we see in Judges
13:1-5. When God, in the form of the Angel of the Lord, appears to
Manoah's wife and gives her specific instructions about their
situation, He speaks to her clearly about her inability to conceive a
child. In the same way, God is well aware of the condition our
marriages are in, and when we allow Him, He steps in and gives
specific instructions on how to handle the relationship difficulties
that we face. Too often, couples blow right past the advice of God
contained in His Word or available through prayer, instead seeking
wisdom from some well-intentioned but less-than-reliable source.
Many marriages experience undue strain and are experiencing a
deteriorating relationship because they are failing to hear from God.
But here we begin to see a spouse who makes herself available to
listen to what God is saying.

Notice in verse 3, she heard from the Lord when she was alone. She
was not in a crowd or in a gathering, but alone when she heard the clear
voice of God speaking. We too can hear from God when we set aside
time in our day to be alone with Him, through reading the Bible and/or
praying. In Deuteronomy 4:10, God tells Moses, "Assemble the people
to Me, that *I may let them hear my words* so they may learn to fear Me
all the days they live on the earth, and that they may teach their children" (emphasis added).

In other words, when we hear from God either through prayer or reading the Bible, it is God, not us, that allows us to hear what we hear from Him. Our responsibility is to spend time alone with God, praying to Him and/or reading His Word. Our hearing from Him may or may not be in such an audible voice as Manoah's wife experienced, but God has a way of directing us through His words in the Bible. When we allow ourselves to hear from God through prayer and absorbing the scriptures, God's Word will find us right where we are, and direct us through the difficulties of life and marriage (cf. Hebrews 4:12). Both through pastoral counseling and in my own marriage, I have learned that the better a couple communicates with God, the better their chances of communicating with one another.

As a direct result of hearing from God, Manoah's wife received step-by-step directions on raising a child, although amazingly at this point in the encounter, she is not even able to conceive because she is still barren. It is this kind of specific direction from God that strengthens the communication between a husband and wife by taking the guesswork out of what will happen and what they are to do. Every step has already been spoken and ordered by the Lord.

God Centered Communication: Judges 13:6-7

Now that Manoah's wife has heard specific step-by-step instructions from God, she goes and relates to her husband what she has been told.

> Then the woman came and told her husband, saying, "A man of God came to me and his appearance was like the appearance of the angel of God, very awesome. And I did not ask him where he came from, nor did he tell me his name. But he said to me, 'Behold, you shall conceive and give birth to a son, and now you shall not drink wine or strong drink nor eat any unclean thing, for the boy shall be a Nazirite to God from the womb to the day of his death.'" (Judges 13:6-7)

This is a critical component of healthy communication between husbands and wives: actually sharing your life with each other. It sounds a little too basic, but in today's high pressure, dual-income, rip-and-run society, if couples are not "intentional" about holding substantive conversations, they can become separated even while they remain married. Time pressures and just the weight of multiple responsibilities inside and outside of the home, which have couples running in all sorts of directions, have a tendency to limit conversation between spouses to idle chitchat more than to substantive, deep conversations.

Frequently, I ask couples how often they talk, and the response is usually along the lines of "Oh, we talk all the time." On the surface, that appears to be a good thing. However, when asked about the depth of their conversations, they reveal that there is little substance at all to their dialogue. My observation is that a relationship that lacks consistent *substantive* conversation usually lacks substance overall. For example, a couple's sex life will only be a physical act and never a spiritual connection as long as their daily conversation never rises above the local news, what the kids did in school, and frustrations at work. A relationship only fed with mundane conversation becomes mundane itself; it lacks depth, and so will the marriage. What Manoah and his wife are showing us is how to bring God into the conversation with each other by sharing God with each other.

Lord, Teach Us What To Do: Judges 13:8

Look at the pattern of communication in this marriage that we have seen to this point–it is a triangle: the wife hears from God, and she then shares this with her husband, Manoah. By introducing God into their conversation, their communication becomes different than the simple two-way "tennis talk" of just bantering words back and forth. Instead, what they now have is a three-way conversation that has been initiated by God and shared between husband and wife. But what was a real watershed moment for me in reading this verse is that when Manoah's wife shares what God has told her, the Bible does not indicate any direct response from Manoah back to his wife. In Judges 13:8, it records his response like this:

> *Then Manoah entreated the LORD and said*, "O Lord, please let the man of God whom You have sent come to us again that

he may *teach us what to do* for the boy who is to be born." (emphasis added)

He doesn't remind her that she is unable to have children, nor does he judge the quality or soundness of what she said. He simply listens to his wife, and then seeks the Lord for further guidance. Manoah does not respond to her with an "attitude," or by being puffed up; he simply listens. His immediate reaction to his wife's breaking news is not to respond to *her*, but to immediately turn to the Lord. Instead of responding to his wife with his wisdom, experience, or earthly logic, which in comparison to God's is extremely limited, he listens to her so that he knows how to talk to God.

I must admit if I were Manoah, I undoubtedly would have questioned my wife or had something to say, some response to her claim that God told my barren wife she was now going to have children. I guess that is where I get into trouble. There is that need to respond, that need to add input to what is being said by my spouse. Am I alone on this? Isn't this just how we are programmed, that we have to say something in response to what is being said. Manoah, however, teaches both husbands and wives, regardless of gender, how we are to respond to each other, as he "entreats,"[8] or asks earnestly, the Lord for guidance. I really like that word *entreat*. It captures the sincere, anxious and anticipatory tenor by which he seeks God's wisdom. His entreaty is a quick visit into the presence of God's wisdom. It is not a visit or entreaty that needs to be lengthy, but one that can happen in the midst of a conversation. In the midst of a conversation, you can listen to your spouse and simultaneously spiritually and mentally entreat God for wisdom on how to respond. On the other hand, there may be times when you might need to spend some time alone with God before answering your spouse. In any event, Manoah entreats the Lord.

---

[8] "entreat," in Dictionary.com, based on the *Random House Dictionary* (2009), at http://dictionary.reference.com/browse/entreat (accessed August 16, 2009).

Here is a guy that is in tune with his wife because he is so in tune with God. At this point, I'll pause to reflect on my own marriage. Wow!!! I can think of at least ten heated discussions I could have avoided with my wife if I would have followed Manoah's lead in seeking the Lord before responding. The most powerful tool at Manoah's disposal does not come from himself, the power of his own words, or his wisdom, but from God. I believe this to be different from how modern couples connect with each other. Too often, we rush in, answer quickly, and in my case, wrongly.

Then, to further capture the emotional place from which Manoah approaches God, he asks the Lord to "teach us what to do." Just look at all the potential stresses Manoah avoided: he did not heap stress on himself by trying to figure out what they should do, he did not experience anxiety about the decision that needed to be made, and there was not even a need for this couple to argue about who was right and who was wrong. Instead, he began by sincerely asking the Lord to teach him what to do.

Until a couple asks God to teach them what to do, their conversations are qualitatively too small because the entirety of their communication revolves around the husband and wife while excluding God. Too often, we seek everything and everybody but the Lord. Marriage seminars are great, marriage counselors, marriage books (smile), and coaches have their undeniable value. But the couple who says "Teach us what to do, Lord," opens their marriage up to receive God's resource of wisdom and power to make lasting, durable change that has no equal anywhere on earth.

What Manoah did by first entreating the Lord, and then asking the Lord to teach them what to do, can be likened to water flowing through a garden hose. If you crimp the hose at some point between the spigot and the end of the hose, the flow of water is halted or greatly reduced. But when you remove the blockage from the hose, the water flows again. A communication pattern crimped by the stress of needing to have the right thing to say, having to figure out all of the answers, or playing defense against your spouse's response, will be greatly strained. So before you rush in and respond - entreat the Lord and ask Him, "teach us what to do."

Navigating through Marriage

Just before we got married, my wife, then my fiancée, and I were both living in North Carolina, and I felt the Lord calling me to seminary in the Washington, DC area. My first inclination at that time was to go the macho route by reminding her that I was the man in the relationship and that God was calling me, so she needed to follow me. Thank the Lord I did not or I would not be married today! Instead, I prayed about the issue for several weeks. Then, after about two or three weeks, she came to me, with tears in her eyes, to tell me that she had been offered the job of a lifetime in…Washington, DC! This fit right in line with what I had been praying for, an answer from the Lord. Within a few weeks, she had moved to Northern Virginia for her job of a lifetime, and a few months later, I moved a thirty-minute drive away, at Capital Bible Seminary in Maryland. A few months after we both were settled into our respective homes in the DC area, she was laid off as a result of the September 11th terror attacks. It was at that point that I truly learned that the Lord sees everything that I can't see.

I can only imagine the stress and possible animosity I could have introduced into my marriage had I forced my fiancée to leave her mother, family, and hometown in North Carolina for a much different lifestyle in Washington, DC, only for her to lose her job and become unemployed in a strange city just a few months later. But thank the Lord that when things did not work out as expected, and her job of a lifetime vanished, it did not put pressure or create animosity in our relationship. My wife and I, like so many Americans, struggled through that time in many ways, but our new marriage was intact because we allowed God to lead us, rather than either of us relying on our own plan. The point is that husbands and wives can avoid so much stress on their marriage when they "entreat the Lord" as Manoah and his wife did. Lord, teach us what to do!!

God Performs Wonders: Judges 13:19

In the very next verse in Judges (v. 9), it states that when Manoah entreated the Lord and requested that God teach them what to do, "God listened to the voice of Manoah." That brings to mind that old faithful hymn of the church, "What a Friend We Have in Jesus."

> What a Friend we have in Jesus, all our sins and griefs to bear! What a privilege to carry everything to God in prayer! O what peace we often forfeit, O what needless pain we bear, All because we do not carry everything to God in prayer.[9]

It is in these times of simply asking the Lord for guidance that we see Him do things beyond our comprehension. Our reasoning and action plans can only take us so far. We simply don't have the strength or the wisdom to outdo God. For God sees what we don't, and when we trust Him, He performs in ways we could never have expected.

> So Manoah took the young goat with the grain offering and offered it on the rock to the Lord, and He performed wonders while Manoah and his wife looked on. (Judg. 13:19)

When Manoah and his wife sought the Lord for guidance, the Lord performed wonders, or miracles, in their presence. They sought the Lord, heard from Him, and obeyed His instructions; then God stepped in and performed significant changes in their marriage. When the communication pattern that Manoah and his wife used—of hearing from God first, then listening to each other, and then obeying Him—becomes our way of communicating, we open ourselves to the ability to see significant shifts in the overall health of our marriage.

How those wonders will be manifested will vary from marriage to marriage, because God knows what each marriage needs. There can be no time frame given for when or how God will step in, but when we allow God to speak to us and then listen; we should expect change in our marriage. No matter how good or bad things are in your marriage right now, I can tell you that when a couple is able to begin to talk

---

[9] "What a Friend We Have in Jesus," originally written by Joseph M. Scriven in 1855, with music composed by Charles C. Converse in 1868, at http://www.cyberhymnal.org/htm/w/a/f/wafwhij.htm.

about the things of God together, they will see dramatic changes in their relationship.

While the Bible does not specify what all of the "wonders" were that the Lord performed in their sight, it is clear that the result was a remarkable change in the marriage of Manoah and his wife. There can be no sound decisions made, no major breakthroughs for the Christian couple, until they talk to God. After Manoah and his wife demonstrate this effective three-way communication pattern in their marriage, this couple, which formerly was barren, receives a son named Samson. Samson grew up to be a great deliverer of Israel from bondage, and it was a direct result of his parents engaging in a three-way conversation with the Lord. They heard from the Lord about how to raise Samson even when his mother was barren, she then communicated with her husband, sought the Lord for guidance, and then obeyed everything He told them to do.

The Three-Way Communication Pattern in Your Marriage

So using Manoah and his wife as a model, here's how you can begin to walk the path of the three-way conversation in your marriage.

1. **Pick a time.** Schedule an agreed-upon time to sit down and talk about God's Word together. It is important to set aside the time, or it simply won't happen.

2. **Select a passage.** Agree on a passage you will read together as a couple. You don't necessarily have to be reading in the same room at the same time; busy schedules don't always allow for that. But agree on the passage and then pick one or two days of the week when you will sit down and discuss it. Make sure you are somewhere that is distraction-free. You might even make a date out of it, go to the local coffee shop, out to dinner at a fancy restaurant (just do not send me the bill), or a walk in the park; be creative and have fun with it.

I usually suggest that couples start with the book of Proverbs (try one of the good modern Bible translations like the NASB or ESV). There are several things that make Proverbs a good starting point. First, the thirty-one chapters in the book correspond nicely with the number of days in the month. So read according to the day of the month. For example, if today is January 9th, read the 9th chapter, and then the 10th the following day, and so forth. When you get to the end of the month, start right back at chapter 1. I have met people that have done this daily, month after month for years on end, and because it is God's word, they never exhausted the depths of God's insight as contained in the book of Proverbs. Second, the structure of Proverbs is somewhat different from other books in the Bible. Instead of one theme, there are at least forty-five topics addressed in the book of Proverbs. It does not build concept upon concept, as some of the other books; instead it is a collection of wise sayings, where one verse does not necessarily have any relation to the next. This makes it a little easier, especially early on, to grab hold of talking points and begin discussing them.

You may also want to try the Psalms. They capture the emotions of people going through a range of relatable experiences. On top of that, the psalmists hang their hearts on their sleeves with an emotional rawness and openness that is certain to evoke spirited conversation between husbands and wives.

Once a couple selects a passage, what normally happens is, over time, other books of the Bible begin to pique your interest and you may want to transition into reading them. But for openers, try Proverbs for a month or two, regardless of how effectively or ineffectively you and your spouse communicate now. See if God does not provide substantive topics for you and your spouse to discuss, and watch how God can ultimately change or deepen the communication patterns of your marriage through these discussions.

> 3. **Just talk.** It is extremely important that these con-
> versations not become a Bible study or a time to set
> forth all of your deep theological positions. It is simply
> a time for husband and wife to talk about the passage,
> discuss what did or did not make sense, identify por-
> tions they could relate to, and share any thoughts that

came to mind. There are no right or wrong answers; just talk to each other and see how allowing God to enter into the conversation changes things. The purpose of this dialog is to invite the power of God into your relationship. Allow the Bible to be the starting point and see what other topics of conversation the Lord brings up along the way. You may start out talking about the Bible and end up talking about raising your children, a dream vacation, the past—who knows what may come up! Let God guide the conversation. I have seen couples who could not agree on the color of the sky begin to have meaningful, substantive conversations that led to lasting change because they allowed God to enter into the conversation.

**Think on These Things: Passages for Further Meditation
and Memorization**

• **Hebrews 1:1-3** God after He spoke long ago to the fathers in the
prophets in many portions and in many ways, in these last days has
spoken to us in His Son, whom He appointed heir of all things,
through whom also He made the world. And He is the radiance of His
glory and the exact representation of His nature, and upholds all
things by the word of His power. When He had made purification of
sins, He sat down at the right hand of Majesty on high. (emphasis
added)

• **Isaiah 55:8-9** For my thoughts are not your thoughts, neither are
your ways my ways, declares the LORD. As the heavens are higher
than the earth, so are my ways higher than your ways and my
thoughts than your thoughts.

• **Proverbs 25:14** Like clouds and wind without rain Is a man who
boasts of his gifts falsely.

• **Deuteronomy 4:35-36** To you it was shown that you might know
that the LORD, He is God; there is no other besides Him. Out of the
heavens He let you hear His voice to discipline you; and on earth He
let you see His great fire, and you heard His words from the midst of
the fire.

• **Psalm 28:1-2** To You, O LORD, I call; My rock, do not be deaf to
me, For if You are silent to me, I will become like those who go
down to the pit. Hear the voice of my supplications when I cry to You
for help, When I lift up my hands toward Your holy sanctuary.

• **Proverbs 15:1-7** A gentle answer turns away wrath, But a harsh
word stirs up anger. The tongue of the wise makes knowledge acceptable, But the mouth of fools spouts folly. The eyes of the LORD
are in every place, Watching the evil and the good. A soothing tongue
is a tree of life, But perversion in it crushes the spirit. A fool rejects

his father's discipline, But he who regards reproof is sensible. Great wealth is in the house of the righteous, But trouble is in the income of the wicked. The lips of the wise spread knowledge, But the hearts of fools are not so.

* **Proverbs 25:11** Like apples of gold in settings of silver, Is a word spoken in right circumstances.

* **Colossians 4:6** Let your conversation be always full of grace, seasoned with salt, so that you may know how to answer everyone.

* **Ephesians 4:25-30** Therefore, laying aside falsehood, SPEAK TRUTH EACH ONE of you WITH HIS NEIGHBOR, for we are members of one another. BE ANGRY, AND yet DO NOT SIN; do not let the sun go down on your anger, and do not give the devil an opportunity. He who steals must steal no longer; but rather he must labor, performing with his own hands what is good, so that he will have something to share with one who has need. Let no unwholesome word proceed from your mouth, but only such a word as is good for edification according to the need of the moment, so that it will give grace to those who hear. Do not grieve the Holy Spirit of God, by whom you were sealed for the day of redemption.

Husbands, Wives, God: Talking Points

1. In what ways did Manoah and his wife communicate differently from the way that we communicate?

2. What areas do we struggle to talk about? Why do you think that is?

3. How might allowing God to enter into conversations in our marriage make a difference?

4. What is one change I can make to improve the communication in our marriage?

5. What time and day(s) of the week can we meet to talk with God as a couple?

6. What character is revealed in the words that I myself speak to my spouse (personal)?

7. What changes do I myself need to make in the way that I speak to my spouse (personal)?

Chapter Five

Isaac and Rebekah: Intimacy—Christian Intimacy

Marriage Principles in This Chapter:
• Prayer Brings Intimacy
• Meditation Through Prayer
• Praying on Behalf of Your Spouse
• Steps Ordered in Prayer

*T*HOUGHTS OF MY YEARS growing up in rural Pennsylvania bring up really heartwarming childhood memories that I treasure to this day. It was such an innocent time, when we allowed our imaginations to run free. One of the favorite games in our neighborhood was a game we called "Telephone." We would take two tin cans, and punch a hole in the bottom of them and feed a string through them. The two tin cans connected by a piece of string would then become our "telephone." Once the cans were connected by the string, one person would holler back and forth into this "phone" while another friend held the other can to his ear. You may have called it something else, but I would guess you are familiar with that game from your childhood, too. For kids today, with the invention of cell phones, our game of Telephone would seem ridiculous, since nowadays, most kids do not need to play Telephone because many have their own real cell phones. However, to us in the 1970s, Telephone would capture our imaginations for hours on end, as we pretended to be holding real conversations. But as much fun as it was, it was really just a game, of course. We were not really hearing the person through the tin cans; rather, we heard our friends only because they were standing just five feet away. In short, the cans emulated real phones, but never were designed to be phones.

In many marriages today, husbands and wives are playing their own version of that old children's game of Telephone. Their physical proximity allows them to hear each other, yet they are ill-equipped to effectively connect or relate to one another intimately. They desperately need and want to *connect* with their spouse in a manner that can be sustained, but much to their frustration, they find themselves disconnected—talking to a tin can.

Conversation about intimacy in marriage between men and women is often relegated to thoughts of sex, but there is a world of difference between sex and intimacy. Our concern in this chapter is intimacy, meaning how mutually open or closed a couple is to expressing their deepest feelings, desires, needs, fears, and thoughts, and so on. Does their comfort zone reach between the lines of their love and allow them to drop their masks, share their hearts, and embrace the vulnerability that permits them to be themselves with their spouse? So often, time and circumstance can cheat a couple of the ability to share their unclad souls with each other, subtly stripping away the depth of love that fills their lives with joy. Over time, the accumulation of arguments, disappointments, hurts, or breaches of trust create walls that the husband and wife retreat behind, as individual safe havens, rather than being shelters for one another. In time, the aggregate weight of marital pressures begins to resemble "Telephone": they are close in physical proximity but yet unable to "connect." As they begin to retreat, they eventually grow accustomed to their points of disconnection as being "the way it is," and either resign to being disconnected or seek connection with someone or something else.

A Question of Intimacy: Prayer

When it comes to intimacy, what keeps you disconnected from your spouse? What precludes you and your spouse from being totally open, and sharing the love and depth of passion you anticipated sharing when you said "I do." Here is the thing: whatever you perceive, think, or know the answer to be, the resolution is the same: *Prayer*. Whether the disconnection stems from attitudes, past hurts, broken trust, financial constraints, etc., the bridge to the lasting, durable intimate connection that you and your spouse deeply desire is your communication with God as a couple in prayer.

Perhaps this is not quite the answer you expected. But more than great sex, or applying methods and techniques to improve your marriage, prayer is where we as husbands and wives connect with God, and He in turn connects us to each other intimately. Yes, prayer, but just not the arduous task of prayer, as it is often reduced to by a sense of mandates or requirements. Instead, we want to work toward a relationship of prayer, between a Husband, Wife, and God, that uplifts the soul, and brings clarity and direction for the path of your marriage. It is through prayer that a couple gains the capacity to connect with each other in both tangible and intangible ways: their dreams and desires, their emotions, physical need, and communication pattern, etc.

Although most have already heard somewhere along the way of the necessity and vitality of prayer, it is unfortunately often described in such lofty and unreachable terms that it becomes discouraging, or seen as being an act of futility. Concerns about the words, techniques, and methodology that are *supposed* to be utilized while praying can stifle the pure heart's desire to communicate with God and can mute the effectiveness of the connection with God. Instead of reducing prayer to formulaic word combinations, catch phrases, clichés, and borrowed rhetoric, prayer should simply be understood as an individual's ability to communicate intimately with God.

As a husband and wife build an intimate communication with God through prayer, they experience a durable, intimate bond with each other. It is to be a lifestyle of prayer that creates a bond among the couple and God that reaches beyond the words utilized, or the perspective that one prays solely to seek God so that wishes will be granted. But an effective lifestyle of prayer sheds the decorative veneer common to the human experience. Prayer brings spouses to the place of real hurt, real concern, and real joy. It is at this point that a couple learns to bare their souls, share their hearts, and risk becoming as vulnerable with each other as they are with God. In so doing, God removes the physical and emotional obstacles that prevent an intimate connection.

A couple's prayer can be as short and simple as Manoah's prayer (discussed in the previous chapter), when he simply murmured, "Teach us Lord," as he sought direction and clarification from the Lord regarding God's direction for their marriage. Or prayer can be as long and impassioned as Hannah's cry of thanksgiving when God finally blessed her and her husband with a child after years of infertility, as described in 1 Samuel 2. Whether long and sophisticated, or brief and spontaneous, the effectiveness of our petitions does not rest in the words that frame them, but in the sincerity that fills them. It is purity of heart which sends our cries heavenward to God, where they find a home in His heart and move Him to act.

Different from the guarded, veiled, carefully-chosen and cautiously-placed words that people typically use to communicate with each other, prayer affords a couple an interaction with God that is free from reservation. This allows their marriage to be the place where they enjoy the unbridled freedom to really say what is on their heart. It is a relationship in which God willingly lends his listening ear and open heart to our every concern.

Why Pray?

Often spouses hold divergent views of the value, need, and effectiveness of prayer. So a good starting point is to ask, answer, and candidly discuss the question: "What is my/our motivation for talking to God?" It is a question that really generates one of two possible answers. The motivation is either because prayer is what should be done as a requirement, or because there is a deep and abiding desire to sink into the heart of God where you can learn about and hear from Him.

If the motivation for prayer is out of *requirement*, then it becomes laborious and arduous and is eventually regulated to just another item on life's to-do list:

✓   Get the dry cleaning
✓   Pick up the kids
✓   Go to the grocery store
      Pray
✓   Cook dinner
✓   Work on the presentation for work
✓   Iron the clothes

On the other hand, when the motivation to pray is to *learn* about and from God, then a couple is ushered into daily contact with wisdom and guidance beyond human reasoning. An effective prayer life nurtures a consistent, stable relationship with God, not a crisis-driven one, labeled "In Case of Emergency, Pull This Handle." Have you ever had a friend, or known someone, who only called when they were in a jam or needed a favor? I think of the expression, "fair-weather friends," which describes people who have a very shallow commitment to a relationship. When things are easy, they are right there to enjoy the good times, but when times get tough and their friendship actually costs them something, they don't stick around—they are very superficial. Typically, that friendship does not last very long.

Similarly, fair-weather marriages that only reach out to God for quick fixes fall short of the type of relationship God designed us to have with Him. Rather, a marriage rooted in the perspective that a constant communication with and *learning of* God experiences an intimate connection between the Husband, Wife, and their God. An attempt at intimacy *only* between husband and wife is no more than human kindness, and in time that ship will run aground amidst a myriad of pressures, as well as physical and biological changes. On the other hand, an intimate relationship between Husbands, Wives, and God that not just includes, but revolves around, intimate prayer with God gains a sense of balance that allows them to thrive under pressure. There will be always barriers to understanding one's spouse until we seek under-standing from God, The Creator of All.

An old mentor used to say, "If you knew how to fix it yourself, you would have fixed it a long time ago." In many of our marriages, we languish in flux, forging ahead as less than fulfilled because we are looking for answers in the wrong place. However, a regular habit of submitting the questions of marriage; and bringing you and your spouse's inadequacies to the One who really has the answers, satisfies the longings and curiosities of the soul. Jesus says it this way to his disciples in Matthew 11:29: "Take My yoke upon you and learn from Me, for I am gentle and humble in heart, and YOU WILL FIND REST FOR YOUR SOULS." It is this same encouragement that applies to your marriage: hook up with Jesus, learn of Him, and find the rest for the collective soul of your marriage.

Pray to Learn

Some years back I spent a few months with an engaged couple who really wanted to abstain from sex during their eight-month engagement period. It was a real struggle for them both, but perhaps more so for the husband-to-be than for his fiancée. He desperately wanted to be obedient to God but between his physical attraction to his fiancée and his "needs," it was a struggle. With about six more months to go before the wedding, he confessed how deeply frustrated he was with both his bride-to-be and with God. It was a frustration born out of his perspective on sex, manhood, and acceptance in a relationship. His frustration had begun to drive two wedges into this romance. One wedge was between the couple, and another wedge was between the couple and their relationship with God.

For her part, the bride-to-be felt that she was in a no-win situation. Her deep convictions assured her that abstaining was the best thing to do; however, she too wrestled with her attraction to her fiancé, as well as not wanting to hurt his feelings. So we talked about a few possible solutions and together we came up with a strategy for overcoming their urges and, particularly, his struggle with this issue. The plan was that they would begin to pray about it for each other on a daily basis, holding their mutual frustrations before the Lord. It was a plan that required shared submission to God in order to be effective. She had to demonstrate a love for both God and her fiancé by setting aside a portion of her busy day to pray to God for him. Her prayer was specifically that she be given the ability to be a source of encouragement and strength for her fiancé as he struggled to obey God and to abstain from the physical act of sex until God untied them spiritually in marriage.

On the other hand, the potential groom also made time every day to pray for his fiancée as well as himself. His particular questions to God focused on the ability to understand his feelings, the strength to be obedient, and learning to trust God more than his physical needs.

As they began to seek God, their conversation with each other slowly softened and they discovered that as their intimacy with their Lord deepened, so did their intimacy with one another. It was their connection with God that allowed them to learn of Him and inevitably of each other. And what they learned of one another's strength, character, and commitment led to a deeper, more intimate, and vulnerable merging of souls as one flesh. Where conversations had been marked by barbs, hurtful comments, and sarcasm, it was replaced by encouragement and support for each other. In time, each began to see the predicament of his or her mate more clearly. The more God clarified their unique individual struggles, as well as those of their partner, the more they were able to embrace a deeper level of compassion for each other.

God began to change their individual perspective of God, themselves, and their relationship in a positive way. The groom gained a deeper perspective on his bride, seeing her as a holy woman of God, and his love for her grew accordingly. And as he embraced his wife soul to soul, the intimate perspective he gained through prayer afforded him the strength to abstain when he previously thought it was impossible. She saw his character and desire to follow God even when many would not be willing or able to abstain from sex in a relationship. Her new insight moved her into a deeper relationship with God and her fiancé.

This couple became so encouraged by what they saw God doing in their relationship that they decided to further deepen their connection with God. So, once a week, they would even skip lunch and dinner, sharing a spiritual fast and intentionally making more time to pray for the strength necessary to triumph through this issue. Throughout the months, as God drew them closer to Him, they continued to be drawn closer to each other.

By the Grace of God, what began as a harsh, intensely frustrating conflict that was threatening their future together developed into a solid marriage resting on a bedrock of mutual trust, dependence on God, and each other. As their wedding day drew near, the couple enjoyed a healthy pride and sense of accomplishment, in that their obedience to God bore such rich fruit. Their mutual prayers for one another taught them how to walk side by side and travel through a conflict-ridden and potentially destructive minefield together. As they unleashed God's strength to trump their desires, they also unleashed their own strength through their shared vulnerability and dependency on God. Thus, their love forged a critical connection between God and each other. The bond led to the realization that their mutual weakness and intimacy brought about a trust that never could have been risked or achieved without the power of God through prayer.

This same strength through vulnerability, which these two precious people found through their relationship with God, is available for all marriages, including the marriages we have looked at thus far. How might things have been different if Jacob and Leah's first response was to reach out to God in prayer? Or would Job's season of suffering have run a different course if his wife had sought the Lord in desperate prayer, rather than bitterly demanding that he curse God and die? Just as these marriages could have been different by seeking the wisdom of the Lord, so too can your marriage still be strengthened and directed by God—*pray to learn.*

This understanding of receiving strength for marriages via a relationship of prayer is found in the biblical marriage of Isaac and Rebekah. As a husband and wife, they practiced a shared perspective of prayer. When they came into the presence of God, it was to learn of Him, not solely to take from Him. They approached God with their heart in their hands, ready to submit themselves to God rather than with a to-do list for God to complete on their behalf. It was this shared perspective of learning from God that enabled them to connect with God, and eventually with each other. Let's look at how they shared an intimate connection with each other and God as they learned of Him throughout their marriage.

Intimate Connection—Deep Thought

In Genesis 24, Abraham sends his servant out with specific criteria and the necessary resources to find a wife for his son Isaac. When the servant entered the city of Nahor, he saw a woman named Rebekah that fit all of the qualifications that Abraham had stipulated for Isaac's bride. At the same time, but yet unaware that Abraham's servant was seeking a bride for him, Isaac went out into a field to meditate; meaning he intentionally sought a quiet place to *think deeply on or about God.* This was not an attempt to empty his mind, or a transcendental exercise to reach a place of peace. Instead, he engaged in an aspect of prayer whereby he was solemnly pursuing God's wisdom through the discipline of biblical meditation, and achieving his goal by saturating his mind with godly ideas and principles. As the following scriptures clarify, biblical meditation is a filling of the mind that comes from thinking deeply on God's creation—word and work, especially related to the life of the individual.

- Joshua 1:8, Meditate on God's law day and night

- Psalm 1:2, The blessed man meditates on God's law day and night

- Psalm 77:12, Meditate on God's work

- Psalm 119:15, 27, 48, Meditate on God's precepts, wonders, and statutes (respectively)

- Psalm 143:5, Meditate on all God has done

- Psalm 145:5, Meditate on God's wonderful works

Meditation is a very powerful aspect of prayer and our relationship with God that, as Isaac illustrates here, brings us in touch with God's direction for our life. This being said, let me emphasize how critical it is to understand that Isaac was not "thinking his way to success," or actualizing a desired result. He was not history's first self-help guru or motivational speaker. Rather, he was keenly focused on God. And at that time, as he was deep in spiritual thought and his mind abounded with the promises and wisdom of God, Isaac lifted up his eyes and saw his bride-to-be, Rebekah, coming toward him.

I believe it to be more than a coincidence that, as this godly man was deeply focused on his Lord, he was given his bride. When we allow ourselves to fill our mind and thoughts of God through biblical meditation, he provides a change for our lives and specifically our marriages. What really amazes me is that apparently Isaac does not even know of his father's servant's efforts to find a bride for him. Yet during this time of meditation, God provides a helpmate to Isaac that would further the promise God made to Abraham concerning the blessing of his descendants. Thus, Rebekah was from the right place, said the right things, and was at the right place at the right time, all as God had directed.

And again, prayer is *not* magic, nor does it exempt us from life's trials. But when we communicate with God and humbly seek His guidance, He provides the direction and solutions that ultimately benefit us. When husbands and wives strike out, in their *own* wisdom and strength, to surmount the challenges they face, they find their pits becoming deeper, valleys longer, and darkness darker. The problems they seek to overcome grow more distressing and overwhelming than necessary, for they are generally bigger and stronger than the wisdom and prowess of man. However, life's trials are never bigger or stronger than God. In the story of Isaac and Rebekah, we see that the Lord lights a path through a maze of troubles when husbands and wives commune with Him, and take time to think deeply about God through prayer and meditation.

Intimate Connection—Praying Spouse

Despite the clear hand of God in their marriage up to this point, Isaac and Rebekah, just as you and I, still are not excused from life's pressures. But, instead of allowing the pressure of their problems to force them apart, they made the crisis work for them and drive them closer together. It strengthened their connection to one another by communication (prayer) with God. The specific pressure they faced surfaced shortly after they were married, when Rebekah discovered that she was unable to have children. Isaac's response was to intercede on *behalf* of his wife (Gen. 25:21).

Based on the specific wording of verse 21 in the original Hebrew, a better way to think of Isaac's *prayer on behalf of* Rebekah is that he *presented or submitted himself* before the Lord for the sake of his wife. Offering much more than just words of concern flowing from his mouth, Isaac inquired of the Lord with a degree of fervor that carried him deep into the heart of God for the sake of his wife. He did so by praying in great depth and displaying commitment and a sacrificial posture to both his God and Rebekah, and by setting aside his own personal concerns. The extreme reach of his commitment is reflected in that he continued pouring his heart out to God some twenty years without having yet seen a tangible change in his wife's condition! According to verse 20, Isaac was forty years old when he married Rebekah, but verse 26 has him as sixty years old when Rebekah gave birth.[10]

Isaac did not just utter a few words into the air for his beloved, but relentlessly involved himself in her condition, presenting himself to the Lord on her behalf for 20 years. That is 20 years of Isaac seeing no change, no results, but still he kept on presenting himself before God in prayer–on behalf of his wife. What an amazingly selfless act of perseverance, love, and commitment on Isaac's part!!! This wasn't about the cultural stigma borne by a family when someone's womb was found to be barren. That was set aside! Isaac's heart was broken for his wife, leading him to intervene on her behalf. It is one thing to hear or be aware of a spouse's situation but to commit to personally involve yourself is altogether different. Isaac does not offer his own suggestions or remedies for his wife's condition. Rather, he pleads with God on Rebekah's behalf and the

---

[10] This statement is based on the assumption that Isaac was praying for Rebekah's barrenness from the beginning of their marriage. The brevity in which the twenty-year span is covered seems to point to his having prayed the entire time. However, to be fair, it does not specifically state the duration of his prayers.

Bible says that when he presented himself before the Lord, the Lord answered him and she conceived.

Isaac offers another vivid demonstration of how God provides the balance necessary for a relationship to endure marital strain. When husbands and wives express concern for their spouse by sacrificially and humbly presenting themselves before the Lord, they strike a favorable balance with Him. It is a balance that exceeds well-intentioned words between man and woman and *presents* God's power into the deepest, darkest conceivable pains that a husband and wife confront. Unfortunately, this type of submission to one another is lacking in many marriages. The intention and desire is there, but too often people submit to techniques and methods of improvement, instead of to the living God. Through your prayer time to the Lord, commit to presenting yourself before the Lord for the sake of your spouse, with the humility and sacrificial spirit of Isaac.

Intimate Connection... Ordered Steps Through Prayer

As the points of connection between Isaac and Rebekah continue to deepen, we now see God directing their path as they commune with Him. As was discussed in the previous section, Isaac pleaded with God about Rebekah's inability to bear a child. Once she conceived, Rebekah endured a very painful pregnancy, driving her to desperately seek the Lord. When she asked Him about her suffering, He explained the severity of her labor pains were because she was having twins. And not only was she having twins, but their sibling rivalry, which would be the mark of their lives outside of the womb, had begun inside of her. It was a contentious relationship so sharp that it would ultimately find a place in the pages of history. One of the twins would be stronger than the other, and the older brother would serve the younger brother. Indeed, when it was time for her to deliver, she did give birth to twin boys: Esau and his younger brother Jacob.

It was from her prayer that she and Isaac gained understanding as to what raising these two boys held in store for them. It was not a perspective that could have been gained apart from her asking the Lord. Surely a doctor could have told her that she was expecting twins, but only God could explain the intense and contentious nature of the relationship that would exist between them.

Likewise, in your marriage, there are some things that can be determined through natural human logic, but there is also a wisdom that can only come from God Himself. It is a wisdom that allows us to *see* what cannot be seen by natural means. As a couple learns to depend on the wisdom of God in their relationship, they are directed through and around harrowing trials, traps, and temptations. Again, prayer is not a magic potion or mystic incantation composed of words strung together. But when a husband and wife embrace this discipline of asking, seeking, and listening, God guides them through, out of, and away from traps, decisions, and pitfalls that can damage their relationship. Ultimately bringing about a stronger, more intimate bond between them.

At another point in their marriage, God again provided them instruction that was beyond the view of their human vision. In Genesis 26, after Isaac and Rebekah had become parents to the twin boys, Jacob and Esau, the land was stricken by a severe famine. During this time of deprivation, Isaac, his wife, and two sons left their homeland and went to the territory of their enemies in Gerar to meet with the King of the Philistines (who were sworn enemies of the Israelites), Abimelech. Imagine how odd this must have been for Isaac and his family, to seek refuge in a hostile land during a time of great need. Yet, defying common sense, that is exactly where God, whose ways are higher than our ways, directs their paths: to a safe haven in an unsafe place.

What a great picture of God's guidance through prayer. In His wisdom, He will lead us to destinies that may supplant traditional wisdom or societal norms. Wouldn't common sense maneuver us away from those who thirst for our blood, especially when we are in a vulnerable position: outnumbered and desperate? Yet the strength of a balanced relationship communicating with God brings Isaac the wisdom of Heaven. Not only does it direct him and Rebekah to a strange land in their time of need and vulnerability, but it also gives him the faith and courage to press into the will of God with his wife, even though they are surrounded by enemies.

As the Bible continues to lay out the story of Isaac and his family, it says that when they arrived in the enemy territory of Gerar, the Lord appeared. It seems pretty unusual that in a desperate time, Isaac should expect help from the enemy. But the Lord appeared and told him very specifically where to go so that Isaac, his family, and even his descendants could be assured of food during a time when the next meal was not a given for anybody.

> The LORD appeared to him and said, "Do not go down to Egypt; stay in the land of which I shall tell you. Sojourn in this land and I will be with you and bless you, for to you and to your descendants I will give all these lands, and I will establish the oath which I swore to your father Abraham." (Gen. 26:2-3)

So here it is, a time when there is a nationwide famine and hope is as scarce as a bumper crop, and God gives a specific plan for survival to Isaac: Don't go to Egypt, Stay put right where you are, and I (God) will provide for (bless) you and your descendants.

Are there any areas of *famine* in your marriage? Areas where there is a scarcity of love, a dearth of emotional stability, a thirst for intimacy, continually barren conversations, and an overall lack of sustenance: a vast famine that cuts through every strata of your union? During these times it is the couple's prayer life that moves them from the land of famine to the land of plenty. It is in those times that God makes his wisdom and direction available to His people, filling their hungry hearts with His bread of life. The same clarity of step by step instruction is available today! The ability to have a clear direction laid out for your marriage even when your relationship is experiencing a *famine*. One can only imagine what would have been the consequence if Isaac would have gone to Egypt or designed some plan of his own to provide for his family. But the Bible records that they remained in Gerar, and against all odds prospered one hundredfold.

As the story of Isaac and Rebekah comes to a close, I encourage husbands and wives to make a daily habit of prayer:

1. Make time as a couple to think deeply about God–Meditate for one another

2. Tirelessly pray on behalf of each other.

3. Seek wise counsel from the Lord for the direction of your marriage

Closing Thought: Remaining Intimate

Isaac and Rebekah evidenced three areas of intimate connection with God. As they meditated on and filled their minds with God, presented themselves before God on behalf of each other, and allowed God to order their steps, they demonstrated a connection with each other just as they connected with God. I only wish the story ended well for them. However, toward the end of their marriage, they begin to focus on their own selfish views rather than remaining connected to God. The end of their marriage reminds us that intimacy is an area of marriage to be continually cultivated, rather than being taken for granted.

**Think on These Things: Passages for Further Meditation
and Memorization**

- **1 Samuel 2:2** There is no one holy like the LORD, Indeed, there is no one besides You, Nor is there any rock like our God. (Hannah's entire prayer in 2:1-10 is too lengthy to re-print, but worthy of further meditation.)

- **1 Peter 3:7** You husbands in the same way, live with your wives in an understanding way, as with someone weaker, since she is a woman; and show her honor as a fellow heir of the grace of life, *so that your prayers will not be hindered.*

- **Luke 11:1** It happened that while Jesus was praying in a certain place, after He had finished, one of His disciples said to Him, "Lord, teach us to pray just as John also taught his disciples."

- **Genesis 20:17** Abraham prayed to God, and God healed Abimelech and his wife and his maids, so that they bore children.

Husbands, Wives, God: Talking Points

1. What is **one** thing that keeps you and your spouse from being connected and able to relate to one another?

2. Find three passages of scripture that relate to this area and begin to think deeply on them. Then share your thoughts of these passages with your spouse.

3. Ask your spouse what three personal goals he or she would like to accomplish over the next year?

a. _____

b. _____

c. _____

   Will you commit to pray for these three goals on behalf of your spouse?

4. Ask your spouse what are his or her three biggest personal concerns (e.g., job, health, marriage, etc.).

a.   _____

b.   _____

c.   _____

Will you commit to praying for these concerns?

5.   What do you make of the duration of time that Isaac appears to

        have prayed for Rebekah?

Chapter Six

Adam and Eve:
Leaving—Together

Marriage Principles in This Chapter:
- Leaving and Cleaving Defined
- God Satisfies Needs Through Spouses
- Leaving and Cleaving Consistently

GENESIS IS NOT JUST the first book in the Bible; it is a book of firsts, as well. It shares the grandeur of the first sunrise, and the first day to ever dawn. It tells of the creation of the first wildlife, and first vegetation to blossom. It chronicles the first roar of the sea and the first shimmer of the stars glistening off of its depths. Genesis even records the first intimate moments between God and man, and the first words that God spoke to His treasured son and daughter. This intriguing book traces another first, one of the most cherished gifts given to mankind: the first time God joined a man and woman, Adam and Eve, together in holy matrimony. This first marriage is where God initiates foundational truths for all marriages to build upon—truths that enabled Adam and Eve to experience the protection of God, even when the crafty serpent deceived them into breaking their relationship with God (Gen. 3:21). The process of meeting and interacting with this couple throughout this chapter will point your marriage to what I consider to be God's strongest principle for husbands and wives: *leaving and cleaving.*

The Need-Based Marriage

The first marriage, between man and woman, was initiated by God and born out of need. During the six (literal) days that God made the world, He concluded each day by looking at what had been made and declaring, "It is good." That is, until God looked at Adam and saw that he was alone. Then, for the first time, God said, "It is *not* good." (Gen. 2:18)

Since God, who had created Adam and thus knew everything about him, deemed that it was not good for Adam to be alone, He made a helper, or life partner, for him, whom Adam named Eve (Gen. 2:20-22). Interestingly, Adam never submitted a list to God of what he needed or expected in a mate. In fact, he does not show any signs of even recognizing that he needed a mate or that such a thing was even available, until God said it was not good that he didn't have one. God then provided a spouse beyond any expectation based solely on Adam's need. Eve was a gift whom Adam accepted with great joy and understanding of the depth of commitment and dependence that would exist between the two of them: "And Adam said, 'This is now bone of my bones, and flesh of my flesh: she shall be called Woman, because she was taken out of Man'" (Gen. 2:23, KJV).

Following Adam's unbridled expression of joy regarding the specific blessing of receiving a wife, God then broadens the focus in Genesis 2:24 from Adam and Eve to include *your* marriage, by stating, "Therefore shall a man leave his father and his mother, and be joined to his wife; and they shall become one flesh".

We will deal with the specifics of this heavenly declaration in the next section. But at this point, what is relevant is God's inclusion of your marriage into the ***need-based*** principle. For, just as Adam's need was the impetus for God's gift of Eve to him, God now says, *Therefore,* or because of Adam's need, *a man*—that is, every man—shall leave his parents and be joined to *his wife,* and *they* shall become one. Clearly, this reaches beyond Adam and Eve and into every marriage, including yours. It is a shift in focus that lets us know that God not only gave Eve to Adam based on his need but (hold on to your seat), He also gave you your spouse based on your needs! Even in the depths of marital strife,[11]

---

[11] I implore you to use wisdom, especially when physical abuse is involved. Seek a licensed counselor or therapist, or consult your local authorities without delay.

the biblical reality is that God, knowing everything about you and your spouse, past, present, and future, looked at you and your spouse individually and provided you, in each other, all you need. Now, I have never been physically assaulted but you cannot imagine the looks I get when I share this with a couple that is convinced that divorce is the best solution. I understand - in the throes of heartache and talk of a break-up, it is hard to see that your spouse is a solution to anything. Yet in God's truth in His word, many couples have found strength to rebuild in the midst of infidelity, pornography, years of deep-seated distress or personality imbalances. God provided your marital partner to satisfy a need within you.

A couple called me a few years ago and asked to meet to talk about their impending divorce. At the point that we met, the couple's wheels were well in motion toward divorce. The attorneys had been contacted and the battle lines of a nasty custody fight were drawn. They had reached a point of saying, after nearly ten years of marriage, "I don't love you, and I never really did." The only thing they did agree on is that each was the wrong person for the other. Their conviction was that they, not God, had chosen their marriage partner. Therefore, none of this talk about "needs" applied and they were free to pursue a divorce so that they could find the person God really wanted them to have. However, as they looked more closely at what God had established through Adam and Eve, they discovered how their thoughts ran contrary to the sovereignty of God. While they continued to wrestle with and move toward divorce, they began to see the spiritual value of the discomfort of their disjointed relationship. They began to see their points of disconnection as God addressing a *need* – an area of personal growth. In time, they called off the attorneys and began a long slow healing process that previously had been unforeseeable. However, what they did see was that the friction each spouse provided was not to be despised. Instead, their points of friction were to be addressed openly, and then embraced as God's shaping tool.

The point of realizing that your spouse is God's fulfillment of a *need* in your life is that, although we may be surprised by our spouse's behavior, our own behavior, or the condition of our marriage, it is not a surprise to God! The friction, the patience required, the mutual submis-sion—everything that goes into maintaining your marriage—brings about a better relationship with God. Even in the messiest of situations, there is something God uses to fulfill a need in both of you: individually and as a couple. Regardless of how one comes to appraise their spouse or their marriage, God appraises the marriage as being needed in order to effect a greater solution and to make us better people.[12] Your need of your spouse is not always understood in the initial stages of your marriage. But throughout the course of your journey with your spouse and God, He will make it clear why He joined you with the person you are married to.

My Personal Journey to Realizing My Need

In my own marriage, God had to make it clear to me why he married my wife and me to each other. I am now certain that God gave me my wife to effect more patience, love, self-discipline, leadership, kindness, spiritual growth, and understanding in me. That might sound like a lot, but she is a tremendous gift from God with a lot to teach, and I have a lot to learn from God through our marriage. But here is the thing: during the five years that my wife and I were dating, we argued every weekend, bar none. I am not just talking about bickering or sniping at each other, but some pretty serious showdowns. I would say that we broke up about 100 times—okay, maybe only 75. And though from the outside looking in, it may have seemed obvious that our relationship was doomed, we could not leave each other if we tried—and believe me we tried. Every time one of us would attempt to end the relationship, something bizarre would happen that would keep us together. For example, at least twice, my car broke down and there was no one else that I could call to come get me except for her (by the way, my car never broke down any other time). I would get her on the phone and then ask for her help in the most humble and pitiful voice I could find.

---

[12] In his book, *Sacred Marriage* (Grand Rapids: Zondervan, 2000), Gary Thomas asks: What if God intended your marriage to make you Holy instead of Happy? It is a great book that goes into detail about how God designed marriage to bring us as people into better relationship with Him. Check it out.

I am convinced that because God knew what I needed more than I knew what I needed, she would willingly come to my rescue and pick me up. We would then end up right back together—until the next weekend. This lasted the entire five years we dated and even continued for the first few years of our marriage. We argued, fought, broke up, and got back together; it was just awful. It took a few years and a whole lot of prayer on both sides for us to finally see how God blessed us by bringing us together. In retrospect, beyond what I understood at the time, those first years were shaping the two of us, bringing me to the realization that I intrinsically needed my wife. It was through her that God worked out (and still does, somewhat) so much selfishness and stubbornness in me. You'll have to ask her what God worked out in her.

Although the beginning of our relationship was marked by constant friction and did not appear to have a good foundation to build on, *God* knew what we needed long before *we* knew what we needed. I am thoroughly convinced that any strengths or positive attributes that I now have, thrive, in part, because God used and continues to use my wife to reshape me. In those early days, I thought my wife had very few of the traits that I wanted or thought I needed, but God knew what I really needed—the gift of my wife. Her personality and the friction in our marriage helped cut away at rough edges I did not even know existed, and then mold me into someone God could use. Now we enjoy a healthy marriage: not perfect, but joined to each other and able to connect with God's wisdom and power to continually transform us.

A word of caution: this is just what God did in our marriage; by no way do I propose hardship as a prescription for your marriage. God knows what you need and He will direct the road that you need to travel. It will be unique to your personalities and particular needs that God is satisfying. If at any point God would have told either my wife or me not to get married, then that would have been the conclusion of our story.

The reality is that God joins husbands and wives together, fully aware of who the individuals are and how they will ultimately strengthen each other. He is the one that is able to smooth out the rough edges of the two individuals to create one piece, joined by God. God knows you and He joined you with the person that you need, and joined them with the person that they need—and you both need God.

Leave and Cleave: Adam and Eve

Based on Adam's need that God fulfilled by providing Eve, He then initiates one of the most powerful principles available to married couples: *leave and cleave*. It is a universal principle that applies to all marriages and it is also contained in Genesis 2:24 (KJV): "Therefore shall a man **leave** his father and his mother, and shall **cleave** unto his wife: and they shall be one flesh" (emphasis added).

Because of the need that God intends to satisfy in the spouse that He gives, *leaving and cleaving* become essential daily practices that produce an enduring marital bond that transcends the individual perspectives of each partner. To better grasp the intention and then application of this relationship principle, let's develop an understanding of the two main components of leaving and cleaving.

Leave

In a general sense, to leave is to release, let go of, or move away from something or someone.[13] Similarly, "leave" in the context of marriage, and as reflected in Genesis 2:24, is to release, let go of and move away from, and move away from external influences. Unfortunately, leaving is typically associated with, and taught as, something that does or must occur at the start of a marriage. But much to the contrary, leaving is not to be confined to a one-time action limited to the beginning stages of marriage. Instead, a couple must leave continually and consistently throughout their marriage. It is to become a lifelong lifestyle of leaving the external influences that arise throughout a relationship. The husband and wife's ability or inability to leave becomes the ground zero of the majority of marital problems, discord, and distancing, as well as the place where joy, peace, and a harmonious relationship rise or fall. As they learn to leave their previously-derived individual dogmas, perspectives, behaviors, and external relationship bonds, they surrender control of their relationship and become spiritually joined to God and each other.

So—What are We to Leave?

Okay, so maybe you are asking: if leaving reaches beyond the beginning stages of marriage, then what is to be left, especially years into my marriage? The quick answer is that we are to leave everything that keeps us separated from our spouse. The "what" of leaving, once again, comes from God's universally applicable statement in Genesis 2:24, "Therefore shall a man leave his father and his mother..." (KJV).

The majority of the couples with whom I share this verse initially accept it as relegating "leaving" to leaving their parents' home. However, there is a much larger and deeper meaning here. The apparent point of "...leave...mother and father..." is to emphasize the significant

---

[13] "leave," in Dictionary.com, based on *The American Heritage Dictionary of the English Language*, 4th ed. (2004), at http://dictionary.reference.com/browse/leave?db=dictionary (accessed June 6, 2009).

importance of the relationship one has with one's parents. It is the very first relationship in everyone's life, and during the early years, it is the relationship of utmost importance in a child's life. One of the biggest influences (either positively or negatively) on all of us is the relationship or lack of relationship that we have or had with our parents. Yet at the point of marriage, God says a man and woman are to *leave* this most significant relationship and be *joined* to the husband or wife that He has provided.

So then, if a couple is to leave this most significant relationship with their parents, what then does that say about leaving other lesser relationships? For example, what is to become of your relationship with your friends or extended family? Just as we are to leave the first and deepest relationship, then all lesser relationships must be left as well. So it might be that the every-Friday social hour with old friends after work has to be left, or that daily phone call to your mother may have to be cut out. Now, I don't believe that this verse is telling us that we are to break off communication or our connection to these other relationships, especially our parents. If so, it would contradict Exodus 20:12: "Honor your father and your mother, that your days may be prolonged." What it does say is that your relationship with your parents, as well as your relationships with all others, is subordinate to the marriage relationship. Those other relationships have to fit within the context of your marriage.

It should also be understood that God could not have meant "leaving" to be relegated to parents when talking to Adam and Eve. In addition to the stated contradiction to other passages regarding relationships with parents, Adam and Eve did not have parents, in the sense that we think of parents, as he was formed from the dust and she was formed from Adam's rib.

Furthermore, the leaving is not to be confined only to relationships with people. It also includes more intangible relationships, such as perspectives, attitudes, behaviors, areas of selfishness, and the like. In most instances, it is the failure to leave the intangible areas that cause the real problems. Relationships with people are easy to identify, but those areas where we are still holding onto a perspective derived from our life experience may be more difficult to identify and move away from. However, husbands and wives are to leave every relationship, either tangible or intangible, that prevents us from connecting to our spouse. So honor your parents, hang out with friends, go to work, and utilize your perspectives and life experiences, but when it becomes apparent that any of these things, or anything else for that matter, is negatively impacting your marriage, you must be willing to leave them so that you can be joined to your spouse. Apart from your relationship with God, all other relationships are to be subordinated to your marriage. This is the *"leaving"* that God instructs us to do, and it is to be complete as well as continual throughout marriage so that spouses can then be joined together.

When to Leave?

When it comes to the timing or frequency of leaving, husbands and wives are to leave every time it is apparent they are not connected (joined) to their spouse in some way. It is a choice that must be made every day, perhaps at times even several times a day. With every point of disconnection in a conversation, decision, interaction, or thought, there is an opportunity to leave some external influence.

However, when a couple is unable to leave, distance is created. If that distance is allowed to continue, it will grow and the quality of their relationship will deteriorate, thus opening doors to more deep-seated marital strain. Those doors cannot be closed nor the strain eased until the influence of that previously-held thought, behavior, perspective, or relationship is left. A couple must remain willing to leave that external influence so that God can join them to each other.

Let me give you a practical snapshot of what leaving might look like. I recently met with a couple that held rigidly polar opposite views regarding their household finances, which was having a domino effect on their entire marriage. Unfortunately, difficulties in one area of a relationship don't seem to compartmentalize themselves, but they spread like a wildfire, until they consume and strain the entire relationship. In this case, the husband was a business owner and a saver, with a very precise financial plan. His wife, on the other hand, and by her own admission, had never formed the habit of saving or exercising financial discipline. Their different styles of financial management had created so much discord and conflict that it caused them to want to leave each other. But what really needed to be left were their past notions about finances. More specifically, they had to leave the manner in which they had dealt with, and emotionally related to, money.

It was not a matter of who was right or wrong, even though that was the content of their arguments. Neither of their positions was really right or wrong, but they were so different as to be in conflict with each other. The real problem was their inability to leave—release, let go of, or move away from—what they individually believed to be the way that money had to be handled, in order for God to provide them a new mutual perspective. Over the next few weeks, they were able to leave their individual past experiences and perspectives regarding financial management, while identifying and implementing a mutually agreeable financial plan for their marriage.

You see, as long as they were determined to hold on to their individual ways, there was constant friction surrounding finances, which weighed on both their communication and their level of sexual intimacy. But as they became willing to leave their individual vantage points, they could be joined together on the issue of managing their finances. As they found a balanced financial solution, they were able to return to talking civilly to one another and to put some fire back in their bedroom. Likewise, any time an external influence forces you and your spouse apart, it is time to leave that external pressure.

—And Cleave

Leaving is the continuing personal responsibility of every husband and wife. However, it's equally significant counterpart, *cleaving*, is performed by God. In fact, the conjunction "and" preceding "cleave" clarifies that it is contingent upon a couple first leaving. The two components of this principle are inextricably linked: if a couple truly leaves, they will cleave to one another. The two words are in a dependent relationship; one does not occur without the other.

"Cleave" conveys the idea of affixing, sticking close to, or adhering to.[14] In our modern vernacular, cleave is synonymous with "join." However, the nature of the joining is that of forming a permanent bond. Accepting and allowing God to "cleave" (join) your marriage makes it significantly stronger than joining an internet social networking site, the local health club, or an organization where the connection is usually limited to only the points of common interest, and often only for a certain time period. Rather, the joining associated with cleaving in marriage is God's complete and permanent merging or fusing of two people together in all aspects of their life.

The permanence and durability of cleaving as it occurs in marriage is analogous to the work of a welder fusing two pieces of metal together. Of course, the weld can be undone, but the welder's intention is for his work to be permanent. In order to separate the work of the welder, one must greatly alter, and in many cases destroy, the original pieces. In much the same way, a couple's ability to allow God to join them together in every aspect of their marriage produces an inseparable unit.

At the place where the welder joins the two pieces into one unit, they are strong enough to endure whatever stressful environment or elements of nature they are placed into. To ensure the metal's durability, the welder heats and melts a filler material. The melted filler, called a weld pool, is then applied between the two pieces being joined. It is this filler material that actually becomes the permanent and durable bond between the two pieces.[15] In the same manner, during a marriage, when a couple leaves previously held relationships, perspectives, and behaviors, and cleaves to each other, God provides the bonding agent that produces a durable single unit. God's bonding agent is both durable enough and permanent enough to keep them joined in the face of the

---

[14] "cleave," in Dictionary.com, based on the *American Heritage Dictionary of the English Language*, 4th ed. (2009), at http://dictionary.reference.com/browse/cleave (accessed June 6, 2009).

[15] "welding," in *Wikipedia: The Free Encyclopedia*, at http://en.wikipedia.org/w/index.php?title=Welding&oldid=294375737 (accessed June 4, 2009).

pressures and stresses they will encounter. Those pressures may include financial distress, financial infidelity, adultery, lying, miscommunication, irresponsibility, shift of commitment level, addictions, personality quirks, parenting, verbal abuse, physical abuse, loss of employment, sickness, hormonal changes, etc. However pressure manifests itself in a relationship, God's bonding agent consists of the highest quality material that can and will keep you and your spouse joined.

The durability and permanence of cleaving results in this reality for marriages. If you leave other relationships, behaviors, thoughts, perspectives, and habits in order to be joined to your spouse, your marriage cannot fail. I know that's a pretty audacious statement, but before you start asking for your money back for this book, look at the words of Jesus in Matthew 19:5. When he was being questioned about valid reasons for divorce, Jesus responded by quoting the same words of Genesis 2:24, "FOR THIS REASON A MAN SHALL LEAVE HIS FATHER AND MOTHER AND BE JOINED TO HIS WIFE, AND THE TWO SHALL BECOME ONE FLESH."[16] The word "joined" in this verse is intended to convey two ideas. The use of the word joined in this context refers to God as both the source and the glue or adhesive that keeps a couple together. It is a liberating and empowering understanding that reminds couples that God is both the one that does the joining and also the adhesive that keeps them together. It is a perspective that can lift a mountain's worth of stress off of a couple! Just as neither the husband nor the wife performed the ceremony in which they were married, so they are not the ones that keep themselves together, either. Rather, God has joined them together and God is also the glue that keeps them together.

Then, in the very next verse, Jesus says, "So they are no longer two, but one flesh. What therefore God has joined together, let no man separate" (Matt. 19:6). In this verse, the word that is being used for

---

[16] The words in this verse are in all capital letters in the New American Standard Bible to indicate a direct quote.

"joined" refers to an inseparable bond or seal.[17] I liken it to the seal of an envelope. I tried many times as a child to open envelopes that my school sent home to my parents, but I quickly learned, and re-learned through my father's stern correction that you can't successfully unseal and then reseal an envelope without the envelope being altered. In the same way, the seal that God puts on a marriage when He joins it can't be broken without damaging the original. Again, we are to take comfort in the fact that God is the one that seals a marriage and, according to this verse, when it is sealed there is no one that can unseal it.

If, according to Matthew 19:5-6, God is the one that joins a couple, and is the glue that keeps them together and no man can separate them, then when a marriage becomes un-joined or divorced in some way, it means that the husband and wife were not truly joined in some area. According to the Bible, it is not possible for a marriage to become unglued by an external entity. So then, where difficulties and distance persist between spouses, the encouragement is for them to look at what either of them has not "left." Some couples who are considering divorce have the ability to look at their relationship and ask, "What has not been left?" Each time this has happened, what has occurred in that they have been able to identify an area in which they were unable to let go of something, either tangible or intangible, from outside of the relationship. So let me give you this question as a gift for your marriage the next time the marriage become strained: What perspective, behavior, thought, action, or relationship with family, a job, friends or things, have I not left?

After having looked at the attributes of these two words, leave and cleave, the precise definition of leave and cleave becomes: *to release, let go of, or move away from external influences, and then, to become permanently fused, joined, and kept close to your spouse by God.*

Thankfully, God intends leave and cleave to be much more of a lifestyle than a wordplay—a lifestyle of leaving external influences and

---

[17] The original Greek language, from which the English New Testament is translated, uses the word κολληθ σεται in verse 5, and συν ζευξεν in verse 6. Both are translated as "joined."

being joined together so that a couple can temper their thoughts, perspectives, and actions in order to surrender to God and one another. So that you can pick the words "leave" and "cleave" up off the pages of the Bible and apply them to your marriage the way God intended; give deep consideration to the ways in which leaving and cleaving nourishes and brings balance to your marriage.

What Keeps A Marriage Unjoined?

If God's intention is for the couples He joins together not to be separated, then the question becomes, "What keeps a marriage from being joined?" Well, let me commit the ultimate no-no by answering a question with a question—a question that couples facing severe marital strain must ask themselves: "What am I more married to?"

Are you married to a past perspective, a past relationship, or a past experience? Or are you married to God so that you can be married to your spouse? If you are married more to God than to anything else, then He will join you to your spouse and your marriage will have the durability to endure the pressures of life. That is the balanced relationship that every marriage needs in order to survive. However, if there are areas where you are married more to your perspectives and behaviors, then you will not be able to be joined to your spouse in those areas. It is not a matter of whether one agrees with their spouse's perspectives or not. What is important is that husbands and wives leave so that God can and will perform the contingent cleaving and produce a durable marital unit.

The encouragement for a marriage that experiences areas where the couple is not joined is to look at what relationships, whether tangible relationships or intangible ones such as perspectives or behaviors, have not yet been left. A brief recap of the Adam and Eve story reminds us that God promised, in Genesis 2, that because He looks at our needs and provides for them, we are to leave and be joined to each other. Then, if there are areas where your marriage is not joined, look at what you have never left. Again I caution, this has nothing to do with years of marriage. As life unfolds for my wife and me, I discover areas where I still have not left my old way of thinking or behaving. These are the areas in which we have not yet been "married."

For example, my wife and I recently became parents. This new development in our marriage reveals new areas where we aren't on the same page. On a daily basis, situations arise wherein I am challenged to leave what I have always thought about fatherhood. I can choose to hold fast to what I saw modeled by my parents, or what my life experiences have taught me, but I am not married to my parents nor those past experiences. However, I am married to my wife and I must constantly learn to meet the challenge to leave and then to cleave to what God has provided in my wife, who co-parents with me. This is the leaving that God instructs us to do so that we can be joined.

Failing to leave is similar to leaving the lid off a cookie jar. Last Christmas, my wife, who is an excellent baker and an all-around foodie, asked me what I wanted her to bake for Christmas. Without hesitation I said chocolate chip cookies; there is nothing like my wife's chocolate chip cookies, especially fresh out of the oven. A few hours after I began devouring those cookies, my wife gently reminded me that the whole point of home-baked cookies is the freshness. However, if you don't completely reseal the container, then air will get in and they will become stale. Although I intended to eat them all within the next hour—well, before they had a change to get stale, at least—I still got the point. When a husband and wife neglect to allow God to seal their marriage by joining them together, air gets in and, despite the best of efforts and intentions, the relationship becomes stale. The only way to maintain a fresh marriage is to continually leave the old and consistently be joined anew to your spouse.

Leave and Cleave—Together

The application to your marriage of the principles seen in the story of Adam and Eve provides a balanced relationship between you, your spouse, and God. It is a relationship with God that balances your relationship with your spouse. Here is what you can do immediately to begin to apply leave and cleave to your marriage.

Ask yourself, and then each other, "What have I or we not left that is affecting our marriage? How is my present behavior representing an old mind set?" Whatever the answers prove to be, your marriage can be restored; let God join your marriage. God gave you and your spouse to each other because He saw an unmet need and He is well aware where you are disconnected from your spouse. Allow God to show you how to evaluate yourself (and your marriage), and determine what needs to be left behind. Leaving and cleaving is so fundamental to a healthy marriage that it deserves further exploration. In the next chapter, through the marriage of David and Michal, we will look at the consequences that a couple might experience when they don't learn to leave and cleave.

Think on These Things: Passages for Further Meditation and Memorization

- **Ephesians 5:22-33** Wives, be subject to your own husbands, as to the Lord. For the husband is the head of the wife, as Christ also is the head of the church, He Himself being the Savior of the body. But as the church is subject to Christ, so also the wives ought to be to their husbands in everything. Husbands, love your wives, just as Christ also loved the church and gave Himself up for her, so that He might sanctify her, having cleansed her by the washing of water with the word, that He might present to Himself the church in all her glory, having no spot or wrinkle or any such thing; but that she would be holy and blameless. So husbands ought also to love their own wives as their own bodies. He who loves his own wife loves himself; for no one ever hated his own flesh, but nourishes and cherishes it, just as Christ also does the church, because we are members of His body. FOR THIS REASON A MAN SHALL LEAVE HIS FATHER AND MOTHER AND SHALL BE JOINED TO HIS WIFE, AND THE TWO SHALL BECOME ONE FLESH. This mystery is great; but I am speaking with reference to Christ and the church. Nevertheless, each individual among you also is to love his own wife even as himself, and the wife must see to it that she respects her husband.

- **Colossians 3:18-19** Wives, be subject to your husbands, as is fitting in the Lord. Husbands, love your wives and do not be embittered against them.

- **1 Corinthians 7:4-5** The wife's body does not belong to her alone but also to her husband. In the same way, the husband's body does not belong to him alone but also to his wife. Do not deprive each other except by mutual consent and for a time, so that you may devote yourselves to prayer. Then come together again so that Satan will not tempt you because of your lack of self-control.

- **Philippians 2:2-11** make my joy complete by being of the same mind, maintaining the same love, united in spirit, intent on one purpose. Do nothing from selfishness or empty conceit, but with humility of mind regard one another as more important than yourselves; do not look out merely for your own personal interests, but also for the interests of others. Have this attitude in yourselves which was also in Christ Jesus...

Husbands, Wives, God: Talking Points

1. What have I individually, or we as a couple, not left that is hinder-

    ing our efforts to be closer in our marriage?

2. Ask your spouse: in what ways are we more married to our

    perspectives and other relationships than to each other?

3. How is my present behavior representing an old mind set?

4. How have the difficult times of my marriage made me a better

    person?

Chapter Seven

David and Michal: More Leaving

Marriage Principles in This Chapter:
- Physical Separation
- Emotional Separation
- Consequences of Failing to Leave
- How to leave

AS THE LAST CHAPTER EXPLAINED while exploring the marriage of Adam and Eve, a couple's inability to leave, whether tangible or intangible relationships, in order to be joined is the dominant root of marital stresses. Since the Bible is conspicuously silent about Adam and Eve's marriage beyond its beginning, in this last chapter will dig deeper into the healing virtue of leaving and cleaving continuously throughout your marriage by exploring the marriage of David and Michal. This marriage provides a more complete picture of the ongoing burden that a marriage is forced to bear when the couple fails to leave and cleave.

The failure of David and Michal to embrace this principle causes them to experience two common consequences of not learning to leave consistently throughout their marriage. These consequences carry with them progressively toxic effects that can devour, or at least deeply strain, even the best of relationships.

I want to emphasize, again, that leave and cleave should not be thought of as something occurring only in the beginning of a marriage.

Nor should it be thought of as only leaving tangible relationships with people close to you, such as parents and friends. Rather, it is a way of life that applies to every relationship across the board, even intangible relationships such as perspectives, thoughts, and behaviors. Thus, to get the most out of this chapter, as the points of separation in David and Michal's marriage are highlighted, make a note of where you feel that you are separated from your spouse in any way. Identifying potential areas of separation or distance in your marriage throughout this chapter will prove essential toward its end in allowing God to chart a new direction for you and your spouse.

David and the King's Daughter

David is one of the most recognizable characters in the Bible, and is one of the two "star attractions" in the well-known account of David and Goliath the Giant. Immediately after David killed Goliath, Israel's King Saul began to resent him because of the attention and accolades he received for saving the nation. As David's popularity steadily grew, so did the King's animosity toward him. Out of his growing fear and hostility, Saul extended a rather disingenuous offer to his young nemesis: his oldest daughter Merab's hand in marriage (1 Sam. 18:17). David rejected this offer, citing that he was not worthy of marrying the king's daughter, a wise decision that, however, further intensified Saul's bitterness toward him. Then in v. 20, Saul's servants learn that his younger daughter Michal loved David (cf. 1 Sam. 18:20, 28). Saul then offers his younger daughter to David, with motives just as dubious, saying, "I will give her to him that she may become a snare to him, and that the hand of the Philistines may be against him." (1 Sam. 18:21). Curiously, this time David accepts Saul's offer, and takes Michal as his wife.

Consequence #1: Physical Separation

Although David and Michal were now married, their relationship immediately experienced pressure fro, Michal's father, King Saul. Look at this account:

Saul sent men to David's house to watch it and to kill him in the morning. But Michal, David's wife, warned him, "If you don't run for your life tonight, tomorrow you'll be killed." So Michal let David down through a window, and he fled and escaped. Then Michal took an idol and laid it on the bed, covering it with a garment and putting some goats' hair at the head. When Saul sent the men to capture David, Michal said, "He is ill." Then Saul sent the men back to see David and told them, "Bring him up to me in his bed so that I may kill him." But when the men entered, there was the idol in the bed, and at the head was some goats' hair. Saul said to Michal, "Why did you deceive me like this and send my enemy away so that he escaped?" Michal told him, "He said to me, 'Let me get away. Why should I kill you?'" (1 Sam. 19:11-17, NASB)

That's a pretty intense scene, to say the least. I think that you'd agree that having your father-in-law send guards to your house to kill you would put a damper on most honeymoons. Yet even in the face of Saul and his soldiers trying to kill David, this husband and wife have to choose how they will respond: (a) *Leave* Saul's pressure and be together as husband and wife; or (b) Don't leave and experience the consequences. Regrettably, they chose the second option.

When Michal learned of her father's plan to kill David, she warned him and provided a way for her new husband to escape. David then chose to run. Saul's pressure on the relationship, particularly the threat to David's life, forced him to flee the scene and his new bride, thus causing the couple to be married but physically separated. While Saul's pressure on the relationship and the resulting distance is problematic, it is the reaction of David and Michal that will get most of our attention. For the reality is that whatever the source of pressure, a couple can't stop the events and stresses of life from occurring. However, when inevitable tensions arise, the question becomes, "Will a couple be able to leave that source of tension and be joined together?" It is in a husband and wife's chosen response to external pressures that a relationship thrives or dies. It was David and Michal's failure to respond appropriately and leave Saul's influence that prevented their marriage from being sealed by God's words in Genesis 2:24, "For this reason a man and woman shall leave... and be joined... *and they shall become one flesh.*"

Theirs were individual decisions that didn't seem to consider God's promises for husbands and wives. Rather they considered their individual welfare above God's promises. Michal could have left her father's influence and fled with her husband so that they could have been together. Likewise, David could have looked beyond his father-in-law's threats and taken his wife with him when he left. While no one can ever say what this marriage might have become, it was robbed of any chance to be what God declared marriage should be in Genesis, chapter 2, because they failed to leave, or separate themselves from, the outside pressures of Saul.

It is unclear how many years they were physically separated. However, what is crystal clear is that the distance begins to tear at their marriage. During their apparently lengthy separation, which extends from 1 Samuel 19 to 2 Samuel 6, Michal is given in marriage to a man named Palti, and David marries two other women, Ahinoam and Abigail (1 Sam. 25:42-44). Obviously there are cultural differences and realities influencing David, Michal, and this entire story that sharply contrast what we face today. But what remains relevant, regardless of culture, is that it was the failure of David and Michal to leave behind their external ties that created the space which allowed other influences to enter into the marriage.

The physical separation in your own marriage may look different than it did in David and Michal's marriage. In our present dual-income, fast-paced, highly-stressed, never-enough-hours-in-a-day society, a couple can live in the same house and still be physically separated. A mountain of obligations and commitments outside of the home, all of which seem to be of utmost importance at the moment, makes it difficult for couples to find time to have a meal, share an activity, be intimate, or simply talk to each other. How about your marriage? Are there areas where you and your spouse are separated because of a failure to leave an outside pressure or perspective?

Modern Day Leaving

A friend called me and asked me to meet with him and his wife, as they were experiencing distance in their relationship. In their own words, she expressed, "He never listens to me," and his perspective was, "We just don't talk like we used to." To both of them, their problems were a matter of learning to communicate better. What they were in search of was a set of proven techniques to improve communication. However, the actual source of the pressure on this relationship was that they were so tied to their jobs that they became disconnected from each other.

After listening to their concerns, I opened my mouth to speak. Before I could finish my first sentence, the husband's cell phone rang. As I sat, expecting him to turn the phone off, he proceeded to answer the call and enter into a conversation with his boss. Before I even had the chance to accept his apology, his wife's phone rang. She, too, accepted the call and proceeded to hold a conversation. Instantly, I had a crystal clear picture of their communication problem. The way that the phone was interrupting our conversation was the same way that their communication with each other was relentlessly being interrupted. Their occupations kept them at their respective offices and apart from each other for most of the day—which is pretty typical. However, even when they were together, they were really still at work. Their conversation was subject at any moment to being interrupted by a phone call from the office. The crux of their problem was that they never had, or made, time to talk to each other.

It was a challenging few months, but they were able to identify how the external pressures of their jobs were keeping them from being joined. Eventually, they were able to establish boundaries in regard to areas of pressure outside of the marriage that enabled them to disconnect from, or leave, what separated them and be joined together in fruitful conversation. They now sit down and talk uninterruptedly for a minimum of fifteen minutes a day. In actuality, their inability to talk was really a failure to leave in one area that masked itself as a communication issue, but impacted every area of their marriage, and strangled the possibility of any intimacy in the marriage.[18]

In 1 Corinthians 7:3-5, Paul makes it clear that when a couple allows physical separation to occur, they allow Satan to enter in and pressure the relationship. And as David and Michal illustrate, the longer a couple allows themselves to be separated, the more difficult it is to bring balance back into the relationship.

Consequence #2: Emotional Separation

It is clear that David and Michal resolved their physical separation at some point, according to 2 Samuel 6:20: "But when David returned to bless his household, Michal the daughter of Saul came out to meet David..." Obviously, if Michal was in the house that David was going to bless, and it is referred to as his house, then they must have experienced some level of reconciliation. Unfortunately though, during their time of physical separation, a more difficult and more deeply-rooted form of separation occurred: *emotional separation.*

There can be many manifestations of emotional separation, but the common thread is that at least one or both spouses feel that the other is unavailable or uninterested in them. It is the bite of the real or imagined unavailability of their spouse that causes couples to erect, and take cover behind, walls of emotional disconnection. As the years progress and the volume of "guarded" areas increases, the emotional separation takes hold in more areas of the relationship, until the two are totally unavailable and uninterested in each other. This emotional unavailability is exactly where David and Michal were in their marriage, and there are two passages in 2 Samuel 6 that capture its depth and consequences. The first is in 2 Samuel 6:12-16:

> Now it was told King David, saying, "The LORD has blessed the house of Obed-edom and all that belongs to him, on ac-

---

[18] Intimacy includes but is not limited to sex, it can also be depth of conversation, time spent together, trust, etc...

count of the ark of God." David went and brought up the ark of God from the house of Obed-edom into the city of David with gladness. And so it was, that when the bearers of the ark of the LORD had gone six paces, he sacrificed an ox and a fatling. And David was dancing before the LORD with all his might, and David was wearing a linen ephod. So David and all the house of Israel were bringing up the ark of the LORD with shouting and the sound of the trumpet. Then it happened as the ark of the LORD came into the city of David that Michal the daughter of Saul looked out of the window and saw King David leaping and dancing before the LORD; and *she despised him in her heart.*" (emphasis added)

In this passage, David was so excited that God had allowed him to return the Ark of the Covenant (God's throne, in the Old Testament) to Jerusalem that he began to dance to honor the Lord. Michal was looking out of the window at the same time and, according to v. 16, when she saw David's dance, she despised him in her heart.

Emotional Exchange

It is amazing how dramatically emotions can change as the pressures from outside of the relationship weigh on a marriage. Remember that in the beginning of their marriage, Michal loved David and she betrayed her father to save David's life. But now the cumulative effects of their inability to leave Saul strained their marriage to the point that Michal exchanged the love that was once in her heart toward David for despise[19], that is, disgust and loathing.[20] Michal did not expect to be "here" when she said "I do" to David. However, despite how "in love"

---

[19] Grammatically the correct use of the noun form of despise here is despisement. In order to remain in line with the actual biblical translation it is being kept in the verb form.

[20] "despise," in Dictionary.com, based on the *Random House Dictionary* (2009), at http://dictionary.reference.com/browse/despise (accessed June 15, 2009).

she felt at the start of the marriage, her reality at this point is disgust, hatred, and disdain. Where she was once completely open and in love, after distance has set in, there is now withdrawal and despise[21]. She is emotionally *un*available to David because she is still emotionally available to Saul, her father.

Michal's despising of David appears to be rooted in two external influences: her father (v. 21) and other women (v. 20). First, she despises David because he is being allowed to do something for the Lord that her father was not able to do (cf. 2 Sam. 6:21). This reveals her unhealthy emotional connection to her father that necessarily hinders her emotional connection to her husband. Her unbroken attachment to her father is captured in 2 Samuel 6:16, 20, and 23; in each passage, she is referred to as the daughter of Saul but never as David's wife. Here she is, years after her marriage to David, and her father has died some time ago, yet emotionally she is still the daughter of Saul more than she is the wife of David. It is a point of separation between this husband and wife that has allowed love to be exchanged for disgust.

Second, she despises David because, as 2 Samuel 6:20 clarifies, while he was dancing for the Lord, he exposed himself to the other women in the area. Michal's comments about the other women could also have been fueled by the hurt she felt over the two wives that David married while he and Michal were physically separated. We will talk more about this dancing scene in the next section, but her sentiment here is clearly a result of their allowing other people into their relationship when they failed to leave.

So whether because of her relationship with her father, or the presence of other women in her relationship with her husband, once again external influences impact this marriage. In short, Michal's exchange of emotions toward her husband was an outgrowth of multiple external

---

[21] Here too, correct use is despisement.

pressures on their relationship. From the beginning of their marriage, and even beyond Saul's death, Michal remained more connected to her father than to her husband. It is unclear what the precise emotional pull was between Michal and her father. What is clear is that David and Michal's inability to leave Saul emotionally and physically prevented them from being joined.

Emotional Separation—Lasting Effects

As the story and marriage of David and Michal moves to a sad conclusion in 2 Samuel 6:20-23, a specific point of friction is now present in their marriage: *misinterpretation*. Look at the provoking manner with which David and Michal view each other at the end of their relationship.

> But when David returned to bless his household, Michal the daughter of Saul came out to meet David and said, "How the king of Israel distinguished himself today! He uncovered himself today in the eyes of his servants' maids as one of the foolish ones shamelessly uncovers himself!" So David said to Michal, "It was before the LORD, who chose me above your father and above all his house, to appoint me ruler over the people of the LORD, over Israel; therefore I will celebrate before the LORD. I will be more lightly esteemed than this and will be humble in my own eyes, but with the maids of whom you have spoken, with them I will be distinguished." Michal the daughter of Saul had no child to the day of her death.

David, being unaware of Michal's despising of him, returns home to bless his household. However, Michal's despising of her husband causes her to circumvent the blessing that had he intended to give her. She meets him outside of their house with quite an attitude, before he can even enter to offer the blessing he wanted to give her. David's intention was to be a blessing to her and the household, but she is being controlled by her heart, which despises him. As such, she misinterprets David's disrobing in front of the women as sexual. The separation they experience prevents her from understanding David's joy.

An emotionally disconnected marriage quickly becomes open to interpretation, rather than candid discussion. The space between the husband and wife prevents them from honestly talking with each other, soul to soul. Instead, they evaluate and filter their spouse's actions through their own skewed perspective, as opposed to reality. I wonder what would have happened if Michal would have asked David, "What in the world were you doing out there today?" Perhaps they could have quickly resolved any misunderstanding. Instead she interprets and labels David's behavior as foolish and shameless. At this point Michal is filtering her view of David through emotional strain which is causing her to cling more to their perspectives than to each other.

David's response provides the perfect conclusion for our discussion of the consequences of leaving and cleaving. In verse 21, he responds to her angry, emotionally-driven retort this way: "It was before the LORD, who chose me above your father and above all his house, to appoint me ruler over the people of the LORD, over Israel; therefore I will celebrate before the LORD."

He first of all understands her anger toward him as being tied into her continuing unhealthy emotional connection to her father, Saul. But more importantly, David never loses sight of how the Lord has blessed him. Furthermore, he determines to be happy in the Lord in spite of Michal's view of him. At this point, this marriage is totally disconnected from God, and therefore, they are disconnected from each other. David declares that he will continue to remain connected to God even though the marriage is totally disconnected from God. The final line of verse 23 suggests that Michal was never able to leave what had kept her disconnected from David and God. Consequently, she paid a high price for her inability to leave as the chapter ends this way, "Michal *the daughter of Saul* had no child to the day of her death".

How to Leave

The last remaining question concerning leaving and cleaving is "How do I leave?" As with Michal, the primary challenge of leaving is letting go of, or moving away from, deeply engrained thoughts, actions, and behaviors. Typically, these are attributes that have previously defined who we are. Perhaps for Michal, the lifestyle associated with being the king's daughter was hard to let go of once she married David, who was a lowly shepherd. Whatever the case may be, it is often these deeply embedded perspectives that prevent a couple from being joined by God.

The first step is for both husband and wife to determine the areas of distance in their marriage. Take a piece of paper and jot down two areas where you and your spouse are not connected to each other. This list should be created in prayer for it to be effective. A list created without prayer can only be based on our fallible human logic. Instead, to access the power necessary to create the desired change, both husband and wife must seek wisdom from God. An old mentor of mine used to say, "If you could have done it yourself, you would have done it a long time ago." So spend some time praying for God's wisdom and guidance to learn where separation or distance may thrive. Ask God with all sincerity, "Lord what do you need me (or us) to leave so that we may be joined to one another?" Start with what you, personally, need to leave first, then what you as a couple need to leave. Here are a few items that could potentially make a list:

- We don't trust each other anymore

- He or she committed adultery

- She wants me to be like her father (or vice versa)

- We need to address our financial situation

- He is irresponsible

- She doesn't respect me

- We need to leave some toxic friendships

Note: Typically, there is at least one area that is on both the husband's and the wife's list.

It is best for the husband and wife to complete their lists separately. Once a couple identifies the areas of distance, it is time to assess their individual contributions to these areas. Each person needs to honestly look at what they have not left that contributes to the identified areas of distance. Again, the key to getting a realistic picture of your contribution to the distance will be prayer. Ask God to show you in your reading of the Bible, or through some life experience, how you are contributing to the distance in your marriage. Here are three passages that I personally look to, as well as the questions I ask God and myself, in order to clearly determine my contribution to distance in my marriage.

Lord, am I displaying love toward my wife the way that you tell us to love?
1 Corinthians 13:4-8: Love is patient, love is kind and is not jealous; love does not brag and is not arrogant, does not act unbecomingly; it does not seek its own, is not provoked, does not take into account a wrong suffered, does not rejoice in unrighteousness, but rejoices with the truth; bears all things, believes all things, hopes all things, endures all things. Love never fails; but if there are gifts of prophecy, they will be done away; if there are tongues, they will cease; if there is knowledge, it will be done away.

Lord, guide me through your example in Christ. Teach me how to keep trusting You rather than my own reasoning.
1 Peter 2:21-24: For you have been called for this purpose, since Christ also suffered for you, leaving you an example for you to follow in His steps, WHO COMMITTED NO SIN, NOR WAS ANY DECEIT FOUND IN HIS MOUTH; and while being reviled, He did not revile in return; while suffering, He uttered no threats, but kept entrusting Himself to Him who judges righteously; and He Himself bore our sins in His body on the cross, so that we might die to sin and live to righteousness; for by His wounds you were healed.

Lord, am I being understanding toward my wife?
1 Peter 3:1-8: In the same way, you wives, be submissive to your own husbands so that even if any of them are disobedient to the word, they may be won without a word by the behavior of their wives, as they

observe your chaste and respectful behavior. Your adornment must not be merely external—braiding the hair, and wearing gold jewelry, or putting on dresses; but let it be the hidden person of the heart, with the imperishable quality of a gentle and quiet spirit, which is precious in the sight of God. For in this way in former times the holy women also, who hoped in God, used to adorn themselves, being submissive to their own husbands; just as Sarah obeyed Abraham, calling him lord, and you have become her children if you do what is right without being frightened by any fear. *You husbands in the same way, live with your wives in an understanding way,* as with someone weaker, since she is a woman; and show her honor as a fellow heir of the grace of life, *so that your prayers will not be hindered.* To sum up, all of you be harmonious, sympathetic, brotherly, kindhearted, and humble in spirit;

These are just a few of my favorites, but there are hundreds of passages in the Bible that God can use to show us what we need to leave. As you begin to read, study, memorize, and pray about relative passages of the Bible, they will begin to show you exactly what needs to be done. At this point, you are ready to sit down with your spouse and talk about what you are personally and as a couple committed to leaving. Be honest with each other about obstacles that have kept the two of you from listening to God.

1. Evaluation (Individual and Couple)

    • How do I contribute to the distance?

    • What am I either willing or not willing to leave?

2. Spiritual Relationship

    • How does my perspective, relationship, or anything else keep me/us from hearing Christ?

    • What new course needs to be charted?

Summarizing Leave and Cleave

Now that we have reached the end of a second chapter exploring the topic of leaving and cleaving, it should be clear that this topic is the foundation of a healthy, well-balanced marriage.

- God provides the spouse we need based on His knowledge of our needs.

- Failure to leave external influences leads to some form of separation in a marriage.

- When a man and a woman allow themselves to be joined by God, then they cannot be separated.

- Leave any and everything that keeps a husband and wife separated.

- In order to leave, Pray, Evaluate, and Cleave to your spouse.

—More Leaving

In this chapter, we have looked at how David and Michal's marital strains, as is the case in many of our marriages, were the result of a buildup of issues that piled on each other throughout the course of their marriage. As the years of their marriage accumulated, their inability to leave physical and emotional pressures accumulated, placing an unbearable strain on their relationship. How about your marriage? Are there areas where you and your spouse are separated because of a failure to leave an outside pressure or perspective? Just as David and Michal did not start out despising each other, most couples don't stand at the altar saying "I do" while harboring despisement. It is along the way that pressures and frictions arise and cause a toxic exchange of emotion. Identify where and how you are separated—and then leave!

Husbands, Wives, God: Talking Points

1. How are the ways in which we are strained and/or separated similar to David and Michal's areas of separation?

2. How might the reference to Michal as the daughter of Saul, instead of as the wife of David, have pointed to a problem?

3. What prevents us from being completely joined?

4. What do you/we personally need to leave?

5. What are we tiptoeing around in our marriage because we have not left everything?

6. In what way do I experience emotional separation from my spouse?

Chapter Eight

Prayer For Your Marriage

From the "model marriage" of Abraham and Sarah straight through to David and Michal's mess of a marriage, I pray that some or at least one of these marriages really spoke to you and your spouse and provided some new insight. It continues to be my hope that husbands and wives will continue to strengthen their relationship through their relationship with God. So now, let me wrap up the message of this book with this prayer for your marriage.

Lord, I pray that each couple that has interacted with these seven marriages has been deeply blessed by them! Just as you cared for, corrected, nurtured and rebuilt these seven marriages, I pray the same for husbands and wives today as we build our own marriages through our relationship with you. Lord, you know what each husband and wife who has picked up this book is in need of. You know both where they are weak and where they are strong. In the name of Jesus the Christ, please give them what they need in their marriage.

I pray that every couple contemplating divorce or facing a serious crisis will be encouraged because of what they have encountered through these marriages of the Bible. Allow us as husbands and wives to see that you are not only the God of the marriages of old, but the God of today's marriages, as well. Since the existence of the very first marriage, you have consistently been concerned about husbands and wives, and to this very day, you remain the *One* able to sustain marriages.

Lastly, Lord, I pray that if anyone has read this book and does not know Jesus Christ as their Lord and Savior, please allow them to be wed to the author and finisher of the salvation of their soul – Jesus Christ. I pray that the words of this book will stir up a curiosity to seek you, read your word and come into deeper contact with you. We all have sinned and fallen short of your glory, but if we confess with our mouths and believe in our hearts that Jesus Christ is Lord—regardless of where we are in our lives—then you are faithful and just to cleanse us from all unrighteousness.

This is my humble prayer, in Jesus' name. Amen.

God Bless,

Edward

HUSBANDS, WIVES, GOD: SMALL GROUP - BIBLE STUDY GUIDE

Husbands, Wives, God was written for individual couples, but its lessons have also been used to foster deep, meaningful, insightful discussions when shared in small groups and Bible studies. When couples come together in a safe and inviting setting, they can dig deeper into the truths contained in God's Word and then apply them to their own marriage as well as potentially "turn the light on" for other couples.

Therefore, the *Husbands, Wives, God: Small Group-Bible Study Guide* is a good "additive" to the book. Each chapter of the study guide corresponds with the book and will contain suggested questions that should provide a solid starting point for group study. However, don't be confined to the questions provided. Feel free to generate your own questions based on what you have read in the corresponding chapter. Lastly, I will suggest two rules (1) Ask that everyone read the corresponding chapter from the book before embarking on the study for that particular chapter; (2) By all means-have fun in the Lord.

Each group study session has been divided into three areas:

•**For Starters:** Ice-breaker type questions designed to orient participants to the overall message of the chapter.
•**Principles:** Questions designed to allow the group to revisit and discuss the main points of that particular chapter of the book.
•**Bring it Home:** Questions crafted specifically to allow participants to determine best ways to implement the principles they have interacted with throughout the chapter.

CHAPTER ONE

ABRAHAM AND SARAH: THE MODEL MARRIAGE

Chapter Overview: Abraham and Sarah model a marriage that is built to endure the challenges a couple will face in marriage and life. In the face of daunting pressures on their relationship they exercise three distinct and valuable marks of their relationship with God: *faith, obedience, and a godly perspective.*

For Starters:

> 1. Who stands out in your mind as a "model couple" (i.e. Parents, Grandparents, Friends, etc...)? Why?

Principles:

> 1. What are some specific instances where Abraham and Sarah exercise faith during their marriage?

> 2. Abraham and Sarah obeyed the call of God to leave all that was familiar to them and trust God's divine directions. What was God's promise to them (specifically Abraham) based upon their obedience?

> 3. How do couples today obey the voice of God?

> 4. Abraham and Sarah's godly perspective enables them to endure living in tents, in a strange land, among foreigners, because they

were looking for a heavenly city rather than a physical one. It is a perspective that magnifies the promises of an unseen God above present conditions. What is the value of such a heavenly perspective in marriage?

Bring it Home:

1. Which of these three areas: *faith, obedience, and godly perspective* are the most difficult for you to exercise in your marriage?

2. What is a service project or joint activity you and your spouse can take on to cultivate faith in your marriage?

3. What other tools are at your disposal to build faith, obedience, and a godly perspective in your marriage?

CHAPTER TWO

JACOB AND LEAH: FROM PAIN TO PRAISE

Chapter Overview: In what is the epitome of a bad marriage, Leah learns to change her perspective of her marriage. When she has tried in vain to fix her marriage on her own she decides "this time I will Praise the Lord," by confessing or throwing her hurt onto the Lord.

For Starters:

1. What is your perspective of who (husband or wife) should complete the following household chores:
    a.   Mowing the Grass
    b.   Laundry
    c.   Paying Bills
    d.   Cooking

2. How do perspectives shape how a husband and wife interact with each other, either positively or negatively?

Principles:

1. What is Jacob's initial perspective of Leah?

2. How does Leah attempt to deal with the disconnection she has with her husband?

3. Which, if any of Leah's three external attempts to fix the marriage, can you identify with? How? Why?
    a.   Look at the Good Thing I have done
    b.   Hear and Understand Me
    c.   Let's Just Stay Together

4. How does Leah evidence a changed perspective with the birth of Judah?

5. What does it meant to "Throw it onto" or "Confess it to the Lord"?

6. What if any benefit would such a perspective offer for our modern marriages?

Bring it Home:

1. Personally, what hurts or pains in your marriage do you need to confess and throw onto God? (Individual question, not intended to answer in small-group setting)

CHAPTER THREE

JOB AND MRS. JOB: IN GOD WE TRUST

Chapter Overview: Job and his wife lose their life savings, source of income, properties, homes, honor, and ten children in one day. In the face of the inevitable calamities and strains that Husbands and Wives face, it is their ability to retain the relationship of trust with God that sustains them.

For Starters:

1. How would you define trust in the context of marriage?

Principles:

1. What are Satan's estimations of Job in verses 1:11 & 2:4?

2. Do you think these remain viable tactics of Satan's today?

3. What do you think of Mrs. Job's response to their losses in Job 2:9?

4. If you were facing the same set of circumstances as Job and Mrs. Job, how would you respond?

5. What does Job learn from this trial in Job 42:2, 5-6?

Bring it Home:

1. In learning to trust God to better trust your spouse, what does this passage about Jesus mean to you?

I Peter 2:21-25 For you have been called for this purpose, since Christ also suffered for you, leaving you an example for you to follow in His steps, WHO COMMITTED NO SIN, NOR WAS ANY DECEIT FOUND IN HIS MOUTH; and while being reviled, He did not revile in return; while suffering, He uttered no threats, **but kept entrusting Himself to Him who judges righteously;** and He

Himself bore our sins in His body on the cross, so that we might die to sin and live to righteousness; for by His wounds you were healed. For you were continually straying like sheep, but now you have returned to the Shepherd and Guardian of your souls.

CHAPTER FOUR

MANOAH AND HIS WIFE: LET'S TALK

Chapter Overview: God moves Manoah and his wife from the sorrow of being a barren couple, to becoming the parents of Samson, the great deliverer of Israel as they demonstrate an effective communication pattern worthy of emulating.

For Starters:

> Designate one person to come up with and write down a "secret sentence," without sharing it with anyone else. If the designated person is female (vice versa if male), she will then whisper the secret sentence to another woman in the study group, who will whisper it to another woman and so on, until all the women have heard the "secret." Each woman will then share what they have heard with their husband. The husbands then will share with the group what they heard from their spouse. Is the "secret sentence" the same as what was initially written down and reported to the group?

Principles:

1. What does God tell Manoah's wife in Judges 13:3-5?

2. What is significant about where Manoah's wife was when she heard from God?

3. What can be learned from what God told her?

4. When she hears from God, who does she talk to next?

5. What can be learned from how Manoah reacts to his wife's "good" news?

Bring it Home:

1. What is one area that you can "entreat" the Lord on as a couple?

CHAPTER FIVE

ISAAC AND REBEKAH: INTIMACY - CHRISTIAN INTIMACY

Chapter Overview: Intimate moments include long walks, quiet talks, candlelight dinners, or date night at the movies, and of course there is bedroom intimacy. In every way that a husband and wife enjoy time together they are harvesting a deeper, more intimate connection with each other. Isaac and Rebekah provide insight into building an intimate connection with God to enable a couple to build a better intimate connection with each other: prayer.

For Starters:

1. Are there any funny or memorable stories of playing telephone as a child?

2. Does talking into tin cans connected by a string remind you of how husbands and wives can sometimes be disconnected pertaining to intimacy? If so, how?

Principles:

1. Define prayer?

2. What does it mean to, "pray to learn?"

3. How does a couple become connected by meditation?

4. What does it mean in Genesis 25:21 when it says, "Isaac prayed to the LORD on behalf of his wife..."

5. Isaac may have prayed for his wife as long as 20 years without any visible result. What lesson or encouragement do you take from this?

Bring it Home:

1. What is *one* thing that keeps you and your spouse from being connected and able to relate   with one another?

   • Find three Scriptures that relate to this area and begin to think deeply on them.

   • Presenting Yourself Before the Lord on Behalf of Your Spouse:

2. Ask your spouse what three personal goals they would like to accomplish over the next year?

   _____

   _____

   _____

3. Will you commit to pray for these three goals on behalf of your spouse?

4. Ask your spouse what are their three biggest personal concerns (i.e. Job, Health, Marriage)

   _____

   _____

   _____

CHAPTER SIX

ADAM AND EVE: LEAVING - TOGETHER

Chapter Overview: It is to Adam and Eve, the first couple of all humanity, that God initiates the principle of *leave and cleave* for all marriages. Simply put, if a man and woman *leave* then God will join them together.

For Starters:

1. When preparing to leave home for a long trip what are some of the frustrations or points of anxiety that you often encounter?

Principles:

1. In the chapter, what is the definition of *leave*?

2. In the chapter, what is the definition of *cleave*?

3. What is the need that God satisfied by providing Eve for Adam?

Bring it Home:

1. What are husbands and wives to leave?

2. When are husbands and wives to leave?

3. What makes leaving either intangible or tangible areas of a relationship so hard?

CHAPTER SEVEN

MORE LEAVING

Chapter Overview: David and Michal illustrate the ravages of a relationship that is torn apart by the inability of a husband and wife to *leave* and be joined (cleaved) to their spouse. Immediately after David marries Michal the daughter of King Saul, Saul applies pressure to their marriage. David and Michal handle this pressure in a very unhealthy manner and as a result become physically separated for an extended period of time. Their physical separation leads to an emotional separation where their initial love is exchanged for despise.

For Starters:

1. In a modern sense, what pressures marriages?

Principles:

1. What made *leaving* so difficult for Michal? How is this the same or different from   modern marriages?

2. What are two consequences David and Michal experienced by failing to *leave* external circumstances.

   a._____

   b._____

3. How might have her perspectives as a "king's kid" affected her hardened feelings for her husband David-a "field hand"?

4. What is the significance of Michal only being labeled as, "The daughter of Saul's daughter"?

5. How would you have handled Saul's pressure if you and your spouse were David and Michal?

6. What is to be made of Michal's ultimate consequence being her inability to bear children?

Bring it Home:

1. Which is harder for you to leave, emotional (intangible) relationships and perspectives or physical (tangible) relationships such as those you have with family, friends, co-workers?

2. What would be the impact on marriages if couples learned to *leave.*

Appendix A: Who is the Angel of the Lord?

The precise identity of *The Angel of the Lord* is a question of debate among Bible scholars, because the angel's identity is not specified. However, it is my belief that appearances of The Angel of the Lord in the Old Testament are appearances of Jesus Christ before he came to begin his earthly ministry in the form of a man (Phil. 2:1-11). This is an understanding that provides a deeper comprehension of our own relationship with Christ. Here are a few points that help clarify the identity of *The Angel of the Lord*:

♦ When the definite article "the" is used, it appears to be a specific angel (a.k.a. Messenger) that is being referenced—not just one of the number of angels, but a specific angel.

♦ *The Angel of the Lord* (a.k.a. The Angel of God) is referred to as God:

- Spoke to Abraham twice from heaven (Gen. 22:11-18). When Abraham was about to sacrifice his son Isaac (Gen. 22:11), and again when giving him the covenant for his descendants (Gen. 22:15).

- Spoke to Moses (Exod. 3:2) from a bush that was burning but not consumed, when he gave him the mission to go to Egypt and free God's children from their bondage there. Moses understood that he was talking to God.

- Instructed Gideon (Judg. 6:22) on how to lead Israel out of bondage and famine. Gideon understood that he was talking to God.

- The Angel of the Lord had the power and authority to admonish Joshua the high priest of Israel in Zechariah 3:6. Also, he had the authority to destroy the land of Israel in 1 Chronicles 21:12.

- In Judges 13, The Angel of the Lord did wonders and opened the womb of Manoah's wife. Manoah and his wife understood this to be the work of God.

♦ John 1:18 states that no one has seen God and lived.

♦ Therefore, this specific angel who was alive and active at multiple points in the Old Testament (Abraham, Moses, Manoah, and after the exile of Israel); and who also had the power to judge, admonish the high priest, and open the womb of a barren woman; and whom those who came in contact with him understood to be God, has to be one of the three persons of the Godhead.

Appendix B: Quick Reference Guide

Abraham and Sarah
- Exercise Faith in God
- Exercise Obedience
- Exercise a godly perspective

Jacob and Leah
- Develop Godly Solutions
- Learn to Praise the Lord

Job & Mrs. Job
- Build A Relationship of Trust: Husbands, Wives and God
- Trust God to sustain a marriage

Manoah and His Wife
- Three Way Communication: Husband, Wife, God
- Build God-Centered Communication
- Entreat the Lord: Lord, Teach Us What to Do

Isaac and Rebekah
- Prayer Brings Intimacy
- Meditation Through Prayer
- Pray on Behalf of Your Spouse
- Steps Ordered in Prayer

Adam and Eve
- Leave and Cleave Defined
- God Satisfies Needs Through Spouses
- Leave and Cleave Consistently

David and Michal
- Physical Separation
- Emotional Separation
- Consequences of Failing to Leave
- Just leave